D1061719

WATERCOLOR

with

O'Hara

The Porte St. Martin BY ELIOT O'HARA

WATERCOLOR
with O'Hara

BY ELIOT O'HARA, N. A.

G. P. Putnam's Sons
New York

BOOKS BY *Eliot O'Hara*

MAKING WATERCOLOR BEHAVE
MAKING THE BRUSH BEHAVE
WATERCOLOR FARES FORTH
ART TEACHERS' PRIMER
WATERCOLOR AT LARGE
WATERCOLOR WITH O'HARA

Published on the same day in the Dominion of Canada
by Longmans Canada Limited, Toronto.
Library of Congress Catalog
Card Number: 65-20684
PRINTED IN THE UNITED STATES OF AMERICA

Contents

Illustrations

Foreword

As our way of life brings us more leisure, most of us have extra time to use as we please. Some people fill this free time with games, sports, watching television, or just loafing. Many paint pictures. I had no idea of the vast interest that was going to develop in painting when I published my first book, *Making Watercolor Behave,* way back in 1932. Since then, even world leaders like Churchill and Eisenhower have dabbled with paint, and it has become very fashionable. Now, millions of people paint and it seems almost as many write how-to-do-it books on the subject. Since there's a limit to how many new things can be said on the subject, most of these books are very much alike—except that each is copiously basted with a different author's pictures. Once a man has taught others, whether in a class or by means of a book or film or demonstration, he has given away something of his own thought and has no more right to its exclusive use.

It's much the same as in painting. When someone like Karl Knaths or Morris Graves develops a style of his own and when he wins important prizes and sells well, the country is suddenly flooded with little Knaths and little Graves. Or let Jackson Pollock work successfully with textures and our exhibitions become showcases of outpourings of intricate surfaces. One likes the original inventor more but his work less, because his imitators debase him by doing similar things almost as well.

How, then, can we write a new book that will cover all the things a beginner needs to know and then turn the student into a painter who has something to say with a new approach of his own? It isn't easy. No teacher, book, or example can pour genius into a student. He can be taught technique, of course. I have taught even feebleminded people very good technique. But a good technician won't necessarily paint interesting pictures. He may make himself such a specialist in something like wet blending or collage that the technique becomes all important and the communication less poignant—or even nonexistent. Learning to paint is like learning a foreign language. You have to acquire a basic vocabulary, an understanding of the grammar, and a fair amount of practice with simple sentences and ideas before you can carry on an ordinary conversation about the weather and the state of the world. However, to be a brilliant conversationalist, you have to develop more than a fluency in the language. You have to have something to say and a distinctive way of saying it.

Painting says a lot about the character and personality of the painter. If he has a whimsical sense of humor, his pictures will be full of whimsy; if he has an acute mind, they will be penetrating; and if he is dull, his pictures will be, too. "By their works shall ye know them." It's like a traveler's report on a trip. A will talk about the mountain climbing; B the food; C the women; and D the museums. One will rhapsodize, another explain, and a third ridicule. Many will just chatter.

The superficial individual, even if he has a fine vocabulary, will say only superficial things. When he paints, his pictures will be superficial—and they will be admired by people who are like him. Often a trivial painter becomes a great success because he has a flair for publicity and a nice way with wealthy connoisseurs. When he gets a room to himself in a museum while paintings by such minor luminaries as Matisse, Marin, and Cézanne are crowded forty to a room, you have the feeling that lobbyists have been at work. Curators are only human after all, and some are more impressed by press blurbs and other high-pressure publicity techniques than by their own independent judgment.

The question of judgment and independence of opinion is an important one, not only for the expert, but for the painter himself. I know of one of my contemporaries who can look you right in the eye and say, "I am one of the greatest living painters." He actually believes it because so many flatterers have told him so. Be exceedingly wary of those who say, "My dear, how well you look this morning." You may take as serious opinion what is meant as a polite pleasantry. You could have a fever of 104° and a bad case of chicken pox and some people would tell you how well you looked—if they thought you wanted to hear it. Of course, there are the other kind, too, the ones who think you "look a little peaked," when you feel you are brimming with health. The moral: Don't rely too much on the opinions of others. They can be useful at times, but they can also destroy you. In the long run, you have to be the judge.

Throughout this book I have stressed the need for an independent personal solution to every painting problem. There are dozens of techniques, all different. Try them all. If you have something to say, you will eventually find the means and the vocabulary for it. Don't be discouraged if you don't hit on it right away. You may be attracted to a mode of painting that doesn't suit you at all because someone you admire handles it brilliantly. Give it a try, but don't remain a frustrated misfit too long. Keep searching, and perhaps one of the many experiments I have suggested will turn you into an inventor. That may be all you need to take off and become a new personality in paint.

ELIOT O'HARA

A minimum amount of equipment is necessary for watercolor painting. Mine consists of a campstool, watercolor paper, a drawing board, four large snap clips, an old army-style canteen, a metal paintbox, an assortment of tube colors, a 4B pencil in a metal holder, and four brushes. I can carry this around in an old khaki knapsack and set up for painting anywhere—indoors or out.

Materials

BEFORE you can begin, you will need certain basic equipment. For watercolor painting you don't need very much—just some suitable paper, a small assortment of colors and something to mix them on, a brush or two, and a container for water. You may decide to add to the minimum, but this is all that's absolutely necessary. Before you go out to buy your materials, you should know something about the paper, paints, and brushes that are available. Once you have got some experience with them, you will develop your own sets of preferences and prejudices.

Paper

Watercolor papers range from cheap machine-made papers of wood pulp to expensive imported papers made by hand from linen and cotton rags. The surface may be smooth, grainy, or rough. The thinnest, or lightest-weight, papers used for watercolor are about 70 lb., the heaviest about 400 lb. The most popular weight is 140 lb.

Watercolor papers are sold as individual sheets in several sizes. The imperial sheet, which is about 22″ x 30″, is the most popular size. You can also buy handmade watercolor papers which are mounted on cardboard and cheaper-grade machine-made illustration boards. Watercolor pads or blocks are also available. They have disadvantages for serious work but are very useful for sketching.

Now, which paper do you want? You should try them all eventually and learn for yourself what happens on different weights and textures of paper. You will find that rough paper is easier to use than smooth, especially for a beginner. The smooth papers are difficult to work on because all the moisture from the brush is free to run to the lowest part of the wet brushstroke where it forms a dark pool. The tiny depressions and ridges of the rough-surfaced papers, on the other hand, tend to catch and hold the color as it is brushed on, giving the artist more control and fewer problems. Some artists like to mount or stretch the lighter papers on a stretcher or drawing board. You can do it if you want to, but it isn't necessary.

For serious work one should not use cheap wood-pulp paper because it yellows in time like newsprint. However, for your first experiments student-quality paper is fine. You will feel much freer to waste it—and that's important. Be sure to use plenty of it. You will learn as much on cheap paper as on expensive paper. What goes into the head is more important than what goes onto the paper.

Brushes

Since brushwork is more important in watercolor than in any other kind of painting, it's important to have good brushes that are easy to work with. The best watercolor brushes are made of sable or ox hair. They come in many sizes and several shapes, but most of them are round or flat. Get large brushes rather than small ones. A large brush can form as sharp a point or edge as a small one, and you can do as fine and delicate work with it. At the same time, you can quickly fill in large areas without losing precious time. You can paint as poor a picture with a small brush as with a large one; it just takes longer.

The choice of brushes is as personal as the color of your necktie or hat and you will doubtless eventually select your own size and type of brush. For years I used a flat, sable, long-haired, sign painter's brush, one inch wide. However, I found that this brush was made for manipulating thicker paint and held far more watercolor paint than was necessary. So I designed a short-hair brush of ox hair. This brush has now come into general use along with various adaptations of it. Among these is a convenient double-ended brush known as the Whitney rotary brush. A #8 round brush is convenient for drawing.

Note: No sable or ox ever took a bath with soap or hot water, so please don't subject your brushes to such civilized amenities. Slosh them about in cool water only. Store them (along with your mink coat) in mothballs if you are not going to use them for some time.

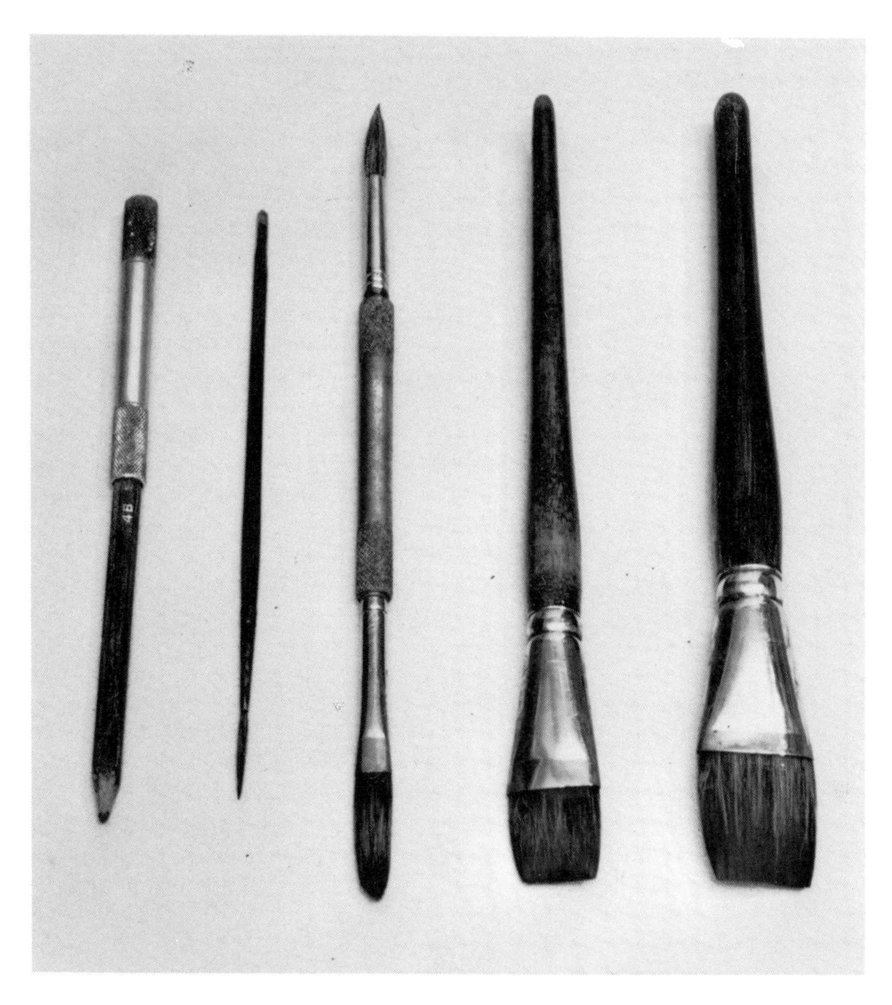

The choice of brushes is a matter of personal preference. My own favorites are two large flat brushes of ox hair, 1¼″ and 1″ wide, a bristle filbert and #8 sable on a double-ended handle, and a #6 rigger for fine lines. A 4B pencil, shown here in a metal holder, is used for sketching in outlines.

Pigments

Watercolor paints are available in tubes or pans in a wide variety of colors and a number of different brands. The choice of tube or pan is entirely a matter of personal preference. I prefer tube colors because the pans seem to collect water, but you may like the pan colors. The choice of brand is also a matter of habit or

The Watercolor Class

COURTESY OF THE ART INSTITUTE OF CHICAGO

Interest in watercolor painting is not just a recent phenomenon, as this watercolor by an anonymous early American painter reveals.

prejudice. All watercolor paints consist of finely ground pigments or of dyes that are held together with an adhesive, usually gum arabic. The well-known brands all conform to certain standards in the manufacture of the paints, and they include the same—or very similar—colors in their lists. Some colors are more expensive to manufacture because the basic pigment is more expensive, so they sell for considerably more than colors that are cheaper to produce.

Permanence of Colors

The permanence of the colors you use is of considerable interest. If you are planning to paint pictures that you will want to sell, give away, or look at for years yourself, you will want to be sure that the colors do not fade. Even if they fade in an attractive way, it can be disconcerting. In a Boston gallery I once saw a Winslow Homer watercolor that had been taken out of its mat. I had always assumed that the gray sky of that painting was intentional until I saw a bright purple quarter-inch stripe where the mat had protected the original color from exposure to light and had prevented fading.

In the past, many of the pigments available to the watercolor painter were undependable, particularly in combinations with certain other colors. In recent years, however, the paint chemists have produced a number of new pigments which seem to be permanent and which mix easily with other colors. Most manufacturers' color lists indicate which colors are permanent and which are only fairly permanent. Some of the colors on the fairly permanent list are extremely useful and are permanent under average conditions.

You can probably believe the manufacturer's listing, but for your own information it's a good idea to test for fading all the colors you buy. It's easy enough to do. Paint a swatch of the color on a small strip of paper. Then, place one end of the strip in a book, leaving the other end exposed to the light of a southern window for a month or so. You may get quite a surprise. If the two halves do not match when the strip is taken out of the book, the paint was not permanent.

Palette

The choice of colors for a palette is extremely personal. We are all subject to changes of mind and whimsies of different kinds. The colors on my palette have changed completely from those I used years ago. The most limited palette would need at least one good red, one yellow, and one blue. They are the so-called pigment primaries and, in theory at least, you can mix all other colors with them. In fact, however, you will find that if you are limited to one red, one yellow, and one blue, you will probably not be able to achieve the full range of subtle tones you would like to get. Some red pigments are rosy, some tend toward orange. Some blues have a violet tinge, some a greenish undertone. Some yellows are light and lemony, others are dull and muddy. It helps to have more than one of each.

The so-called pigment secondaries, green, orange, and violet, can be mixed quite easily from the pigment primaries, but you can save time if you have green, orange, and violet pigments on your palette. It also helps to have some dark neutralized pigments, like the umbers and siennas, and black.

My latest palette consists of Alizarin Crimson, Cadmium Red

Light, Cadmium Orange, Cadmium Yellow Medium, which are all bright warm colors; Burnt Sienna (a darkish red), Burnt Umber (a dark orange), and Raw Umber (a dark yellow); and four cool colors, Phthalocyanine Green, Phthalocyanine Blue, Ultramarine Blue, and Ultramarine Violet; and Black.

Arranging a Palette

You can arrange your colors on a traditional thumbhole palette, in a paintbox, on a white porcelain butcher's tray, on a dinner plate, or on any convenient surface. You will find, though, that it is helpful to have a white surface for mixing your colors. You can place the colors in any kind of order that suits you, but for the bright warm and cool colors most artists find it helpful to follow the order of the spectrum: red, orange, yellow, green, blue, and violet. These pigments can be placed in a row across the top, with the dark siennas, umbers, grays, and black grouped together along the side or at the bottom, depending on the shape of the utensil you use as a palette. The illustration opposite shows the arrangement I now use.

Miscellaneous Equipment

As already suggested, you need little equipment to paint watercolors. The paper, paints, palette or mixing tray, brushes, and a container of water are essential. You will probably want a pencil (4B) for sketching in the outlines of the subject. An art gum eraser is handy to have, so is a sponge or a square of cloth. Other items you may find useful are a drawing board, an oil painter's bristle brush, and a penknife.

DULL COLORS		BRIGHT COLORS
Burnt Sienna		Alizarin Crimson
		Cadmium Red Light
Sepia or Burnt Umber	↑	Cadmium Orange
		Cadmium Yellow Medium
Raw Umber		Hansa Yellow
	Warm	
	Cool	Phthalocyanine Green
		Phthalocyanine Blue
		Cobalt Blue
Ivory Black	↓	Ultramarine Blue
		Ultramarine Violet
		Acra Violet

This is the palette arrangement I now use. Tube colors are squeezed out in the top of my metal paintbox in the order shown, dull colors on the left, bright colors on the right. Both bright and dull colors range from warm at the top of the palette to cool at the bottom.

Every painter has his own way of working. This is mine. The watercolor paper, clipped to a drawing board, is propped against my knapsack on the floor or the ground, with paints, brushes, and water container on my right. I used to like to paint in a kneeling position. Now I find it more comfortable to sit on a low campstool.

Basic Techniques for Watercolor Painting

THE ONLY way to learn how to paint with watercolor paints—or oils, caseins, polymers, or any other medium, old, new, or yet to be discovered—is to get the necessary equipment together and start messing around with the paints.

After you have gotten some experience, you may develop your own special rituals. You may want to put on old clothes and spread newspapers on the floor so you will feel free to splash color with abandon. You may work out some fancy arrangement for holding and mixing your colors. You may decide you like to work kneeling, sitting, or standing, with your paper on the floor, or a table, or on a drawing board.

The main trick is to have the hand and arm in a position where they can move freely across the paper. Kneeling in front of one's work cannot be beaten, as far as I'm concerned, but as one gets older this position seems to predispose one to housemaid's knee and other kindred ailments. I now use a campstool and have the drawing board to which my paper is clipped at my feet. Being righthanded, all my equipment sits on the floor at my right. This arrangement prevents wet drips of water from plopping on the paper. However, the important thing is to suit your posture to your own anatomical peculiarities so that you feel at ease and comfortable.

To begin with, all you will need is plenty of the cheaper grades of paper, a tube of paint, preferably black, a good-sized brush, and a jar of water. There's no point in using the best papers for these first exercises, but it is a good idea to use a paper that has some body and grain. You can work on the smooth papers after you have gotten some practice on the rougher ones. Too thin paper, though, will be a nuisance and will present problems you're not ready to deal with yet.

For your first experiments with the watercolor brush, you can actually use any color or colors you want to, but I suggest using black, for a good reason. It will give you a full range of tonal values from light gray to almost black. (You will never get it to look as black as the pigment does when it comes from the tube—but that will tell you something about watercolor, too.) By working with tonal values rather than colors, you can concentrate on learning to handle the brush itself and forget, for the time being, the problems of color mixing.

Doodling with Paint

Squeeze out some black paint on whatever you are using for a palette. Be sure to squeeze out enough and be sure that the brush is thoroughly wet with water before picking up the paint. Hold the brush like a pencil, but vertically above the paper, then make as many kinds of strokes as you can. These brush exercises may be varied by having the brush wetter or dryer, the paint thinner or thicker, by dragging the brush slowly or by moving it faster, by pressing hard, and by barely touching the paper. Scrub, stroke, pat, smear, and drip. You will have to gain your own experience in brush handling.

You will find that a wet brush puts on a lot of water, containing either a smaller or larger amount of color. A dry brush puts on less water, but the percentage of pigment in the water may be so great that it leaves a darker stroke on the paper than would a wet brush with less pigment. If the brush is clean and squeezed dry, it will blot up or absorb water from the wet paper, taking an equal proportion of the pigment which was mixed with the water. It is therefore possible while the paper is still wet to add or take away pigment from a given area or to flood in additional pigment. The wetter the area, the more the new pigment will blend or run in. When you have done enough "doodling with paint" to get the feel of the brush and to get a sense of the "basic parts of speech," you're ready to improve your watercolor vocabulary.

This is my Joe Doaks house. You will see it again from time to time throughout the book, demonstrating various techniques and modes of painting. Here it shows a smooth wash. The step-by-step photographs on page 25 demonstrate how it was done. For your own experiments, choose a simple house near you. You will be going back to it continually to paint it in dozens of different ways.

A Smooth Wash

The first essential that you must learn is how to lay a smooth wash. There's more than one way to do it. In my first book, published thirty years ago, I described a traditional method of laying a smooth wash that grades from light to dark. Since then I have developed a new approach that can be used for any kind of wash.

On a half sheet of rough watercolor paper outline an area such as a sky or background. Again, I suggest using only black paint which readily allows itself to be stretched through all the values. On a large area, such as a sky, it is well to wet the paper first. Rough watercolor paper is made up of hills and valleys, or bumps and depressions, and it is necessary to fill these, as well as the pores of the paper, with water. Otherwise it will be difficult to achieve a smooth wash or to prevent the kinds of stains that chunks of strong color can leave on the paper.

Now, fill your brush—the one-inch one—with water and attack the sky area exactly as if you were painting the side of a barn. You can tell when your paper is thoroughly wet by the light reflections in it. When the area is soaking wet, dip your brush into the water jar, squeeze excess water out of the brush by pinching it between your fingers, then pick up the desired color—in this case, black. No more water, please. Now add this paint to the skin of water already on the paper.

At this point I wish I could lean over your shoulder and show you how this is done. The best I can do, however, is to tell you how I achieve it. After wetting the paper, I first use crisscross strokes over the area in a sort of basket-weave design. This starts to spread the color. Then, holding the paper vertically, I go over the entire area, starting at the top and moving the brush down with each horizontal stroke. As long as the paper is wet it is possible to modify, lighten, or darken the value, warm or cool the color, or even wash the whole thing off and start again. The ability to keep the paper wet is what makes a good watercolor technician, and only practice can get you to the point where you can do it with ease.

Without too much practice, however, you can learn to get the exact color or tonal value you want, just by adding or removing water. Paint runs out from between the hairs when the brush is held vertically, but when the brush moves sideways across the paper, it takes up paint. Thus, the brush becomes a tool for taking off paint as well as for adding it. Try blending light and dark tones together along a wet edge. You can do many things as long as you keep the paper wet all over. Once it is dry, any further work will spoil your wash.

Laying a Smooth Wash

With the paper upside down, the sky area is first thoroughly wet using a large brush filled with clean water. When the wet paper is glistening with light reflections, the brush is dipped in color, which is then applied to the wet paper in broad strokes as shown here. The color is spread by going over the whole area with a wet brush using horizontal strokes.

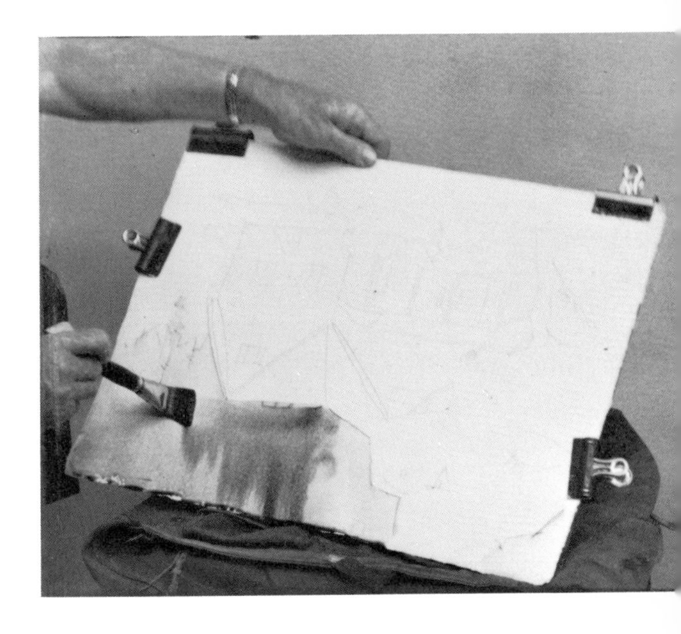

The paper is held vertically so that the color begins to run down. The entire area is then gone over with a wet brush, starting at the top and moving the brush down with each horizontal stroke.

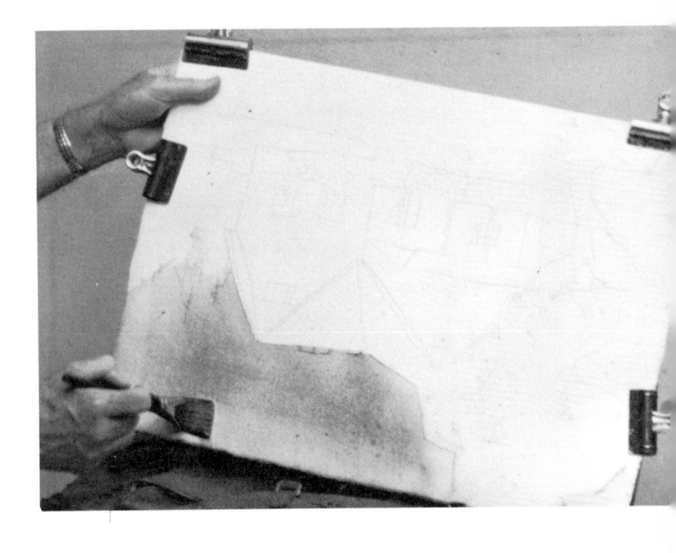

As long as the paper remains wet you can modify the wash in any way you wish. To make it darker, add color. To make it lighter, dilute with water. Before the wash dries, blot up the excess water or paint that has accumulated along the lower edge.

Useful Brushstrokes

While you were doodling with paint, you found that you could produce quite a range of textural effects by varying the way you held or moved the brush, or by using more or less paint or water. Many of these accidental effects can be very useful in painting when you learn to control them. The demonstrations on the next few pages show how certain kinds of strokes are made. Experiment with them until your hand can control the exact effect you want each time you try. Meantime study the paintings reproduced in this book and any others you have a chance to see and try to figure out what kinds of strokes were used for particular effects.

From Flagstaff, Arizona BY ELIOT O'HARA

Several types of rough brushing were used to suggest the contrasting textures of wooded hills and sandstone mesa.

Jefferson Street, Savannah BY ELIOT O'HARA

Rough brushing is often used in painting wet pavements.

ROUGH BRUSHING

Rough brushing takes advantage of the roughness of the paper to color only the tops of the grains of the paper's surface, leaving the valleys or indentations white. The result is a speckled effect that is very useful for indicating certain kinds of textures, such as gravel, foliage, wet pavements, or sunlight on water.

For rough brushing the brush should have water and paint in it, but it should be dry enough so that the paint will not shake off. To test for this, hold your brush over a piece of paper (not the one you're working on!) and give it a sharp tap with your fingers. If nothing comes off, you are set.

There are three ways of controlling rough brushing:

1. *Flat versus Vertical Brush*

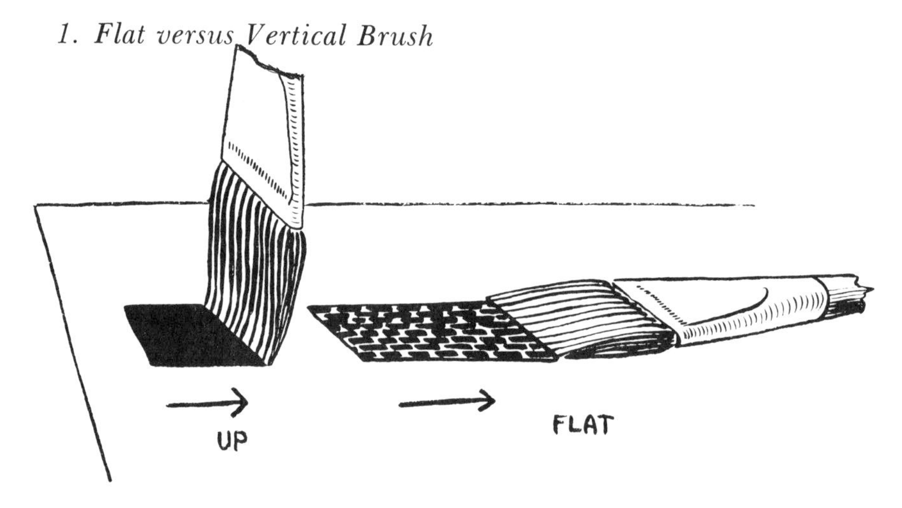

Fill the brush with paint and move it lightly across the paper, holding the handle vertically as you normally do. Now move the brush with the hairs flat on the paper. The second brushstroke will be an example of rough brushing.

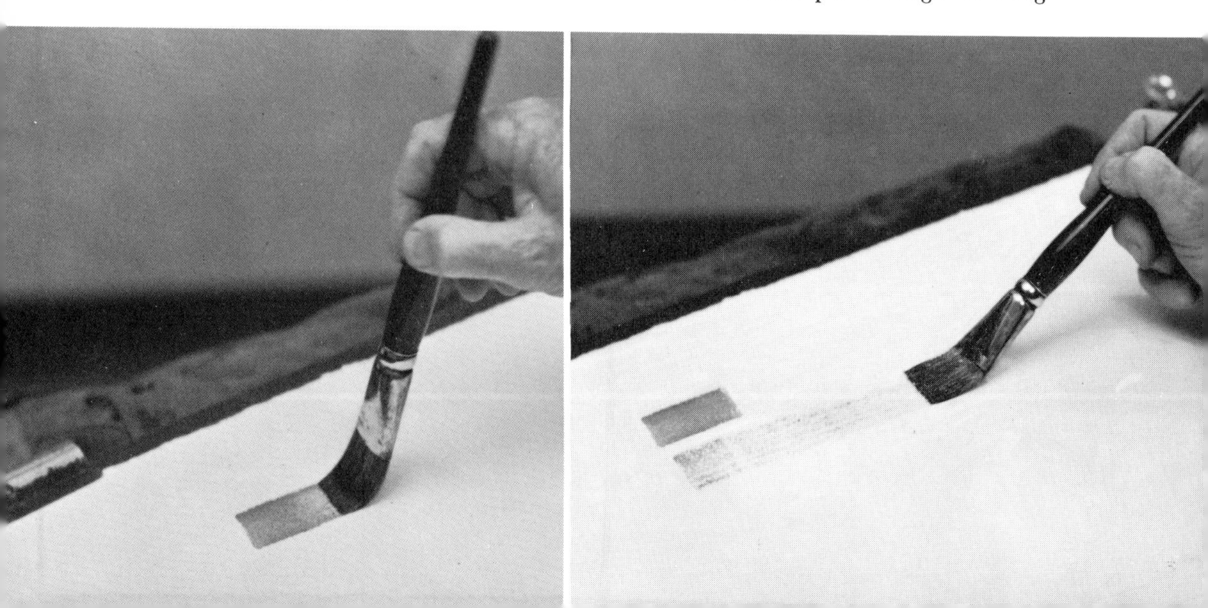

2. Fast-moving versus Slow-moving Brush

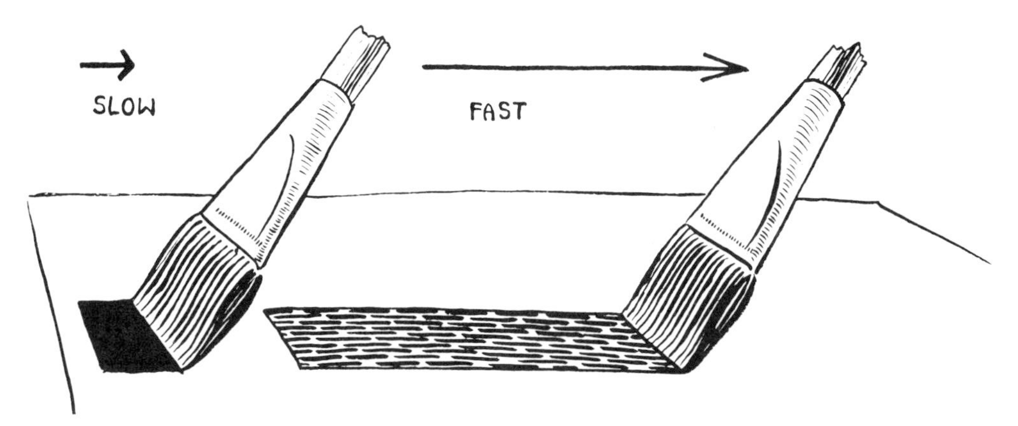

Have the brush medium wet and set it on the paper at an angle of about 45 degrees. If you move it slowly, you will produce a regular, smooth brushstroke, but if you move it quickly, the result will be rough.

3. Wet versus Dry Brush

The amount of water and paint in the brush is the third variant. Experiment with more water and paint in the brush, then less, and observe the many variations in roughness of texture that can be achieved. In the photograph above, I'm applying broken color with a very dry brush held rather flatly.

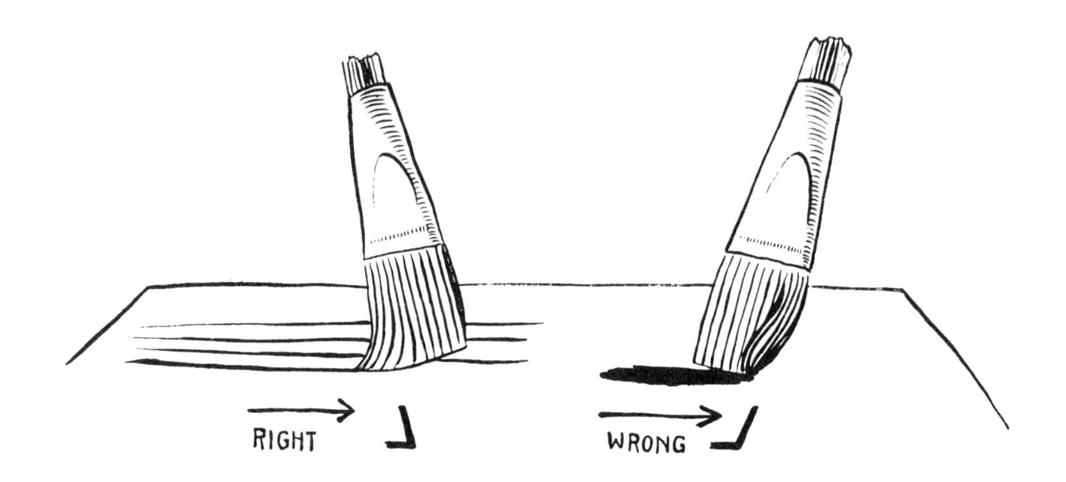

THIN PARALLEL LINES

To draw thin parallel lines, hold the brush like a pencil and, starting from the left side of the paper, trail the back corner or left side of the brush. The hairs will stretch out into a thin trail. If the front, or right-hand corner, is used, the hairs will bunch up and make a thick line instead of trailing out to make a thin one.

Divided hairstrokes can be made by holding the brush vertically and tipped to the left, then stroking very lightly across the paper as shown in the photograph below.

RAGGED-AND-SMOOTH STROKE

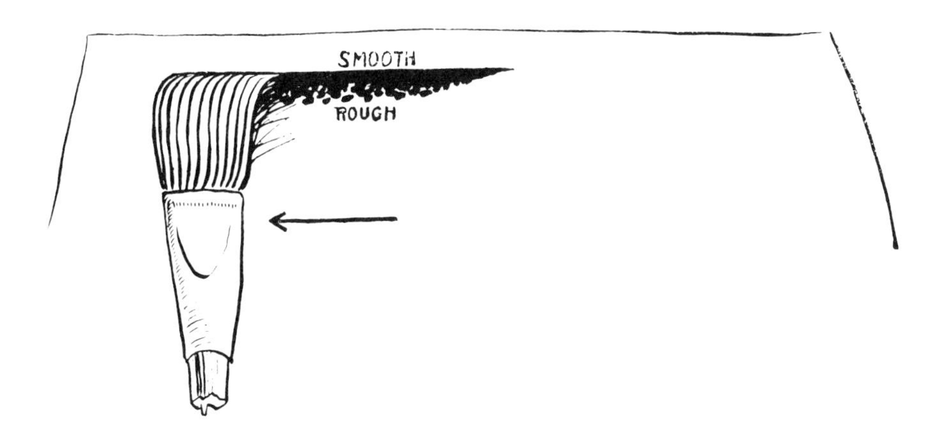

A single stroke which is ragged on one side and smooth on the other can be achieved by moving the brush sideways, with the brush almost flat and the wrist near the paper. The tip of the brush produces a smooth edge on the top of the stroke, and the heel of the brush produces a ragged edge below.

This ragged-and-smooth stroke works better with right-handed people when run from right to left, especially if the paper is tipped slightly away from the painter. It is useful for distant tree lines, the shadow side of a rough tree trunk, grass against the sky, and many other effects.

DOUBLE-LOADED BRUSHSTROKE

A single two-toned stroke—like that shown below—can be made by loading one side of the brush with a light value, then dipping the other side of the brush into another color or a darker value of the same color.

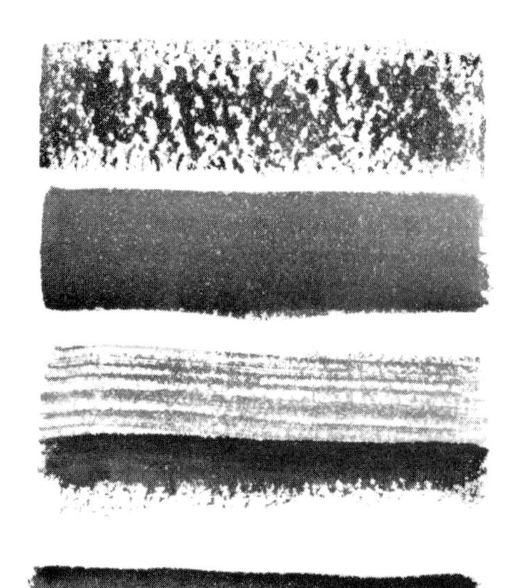

A VARIETY OF BRUSHSTROKES

All the strokes on the left were made with a brush loaded with water and color yet dry enough so that the paint would not shake off. The only difference was in the way the brush was held. For the rough-brushed area the brush was held flat; for the solid area it was tipped. The hairstrokes were made by holding the brush vertically and stroking lightly across the paper.

Some of the many other textural effects you can produce with watercolor on rough paper are shown below and opposite. Try them all, then see how many others you can invent yourself.

CRISSCROSSING HAIRSTROKES

When divided hairstrokes are crisscrossed, they suggest a tartan.

OVERLAPPING ROUGH BRUSHING

Many textural effects can be obtained by overlapping rough brushstrokes. Try rough brushing over areas of solid color too.

BLOTTING

While an area is still very wet with a newly laid wash, blot some areas of the paint with tissues or blotting paper.

DARK INTO LIGHT

Flood a dark value into a light one without stroking. (You might try this with two different colors rather than just black.) Then try dropping a dark value into a light one.

KNIFE STROKES

Cover an area with a wash and, before the paint is dry, draw lines in the wash with a knife. Hold the knife as you would for spreading butter rather than for shaving and use a good firm stroke. The knife will make a wide or narrow line, depending on the angle at which it is held.

Value Studies

One of the great hurdles for most beginning watercolorists is the mastery of values. First, there's the problem of learning to see all of the tonal values from the very lightest to the very darkest and of learning to differentiate between tones in the middle value range. That's hard enough. Then, you must learn to reproduce them, not necessarily as you see them, but as you want them to appear in your painting. And that's a lot harder. To begin with, all paints dry one or two degrees lighter than they appear when wet. So you must learn to make allowances for that. Then, some subjects you choose to paint may have areas that are lighter or

The Joe Doaks House—WITH VALUE CARD

To help yourself distinguish differences in value in areas that grade subtly from one value to another, make a value card such as the one shown here. Use it to check values in the scene and in your painting.

The Red Fish House BY ELIOT O'HARA

COLLECTION OF MR. AND MRS. JOHN BARKER

The sky was covered with a smooth flat wash. Combinations of rough and smooth brushing can be seen in the dark mass of trees, the gray mud flats, and the grassy foreground. For the area of lightest value—where the water reflects the light gray sky—the paper was left white.

darker than you would like them to be in your painting. You aren't bound by what you see, of course, so you can paint them as you choose. What you must learn is to evaluate what you see and then paint what you want.

Again using only black paint, make a number of value studies of simple subjects, a house or barn if you are outdoors, or a pile of blocks or something equally simple indoors. Remember that you must set down the values as accurately as you can. If you don't take this hurdle, you won't make much progress with your painting. Don't let yourself get away with anything. Force yourself to distinguish between very slight degrees of difference in lightness and darkness in your subject and to reproduce them as exactly as you can. After a while you should be able to set down at will the most subtle distinctions of light or dark.

If you have trouble distinguishing values in an area that grades from one value to another, it may help you to look with one eye through two holes that have been punched three or four inches apart in a black card. Looking from one hole to another you should be able to see the value differences dissociated from their context.

In your first pictures you may find that you have gone too quickly down into darks, producing blackish pictures instead of evenly graded ones, or that you have gone too slowly down into darks, producing pale, anemic results. The only way to overcome either of these problems is by constant practice.

GRADED VALUE SCALES

After you have learned to distinguish values, you may still have some trouble reproducing them on paper. If so, it may help you to make a 10-degree value scale. Leave the top area white and paint the bottom area with the blackest value you can get with your paint. Then fill each of the intermediate areas with a value of gray so that the column grades evenly from white to black. If you don't succeed the first time, keep at it until you do. When you can easily reproduce the tones in even grades, number them from one to ten as a guide. Then reproduce the same series of values in a different order. First number the rectangle with the value you plan to paint, then match it to the similarly numbered area in the evenly graded column.

Color and Light

IN THE beginning there was darkness, then light and color. Without light, there is no color. If your mind refuses to accept that, observe what happens to the color or colors of any object as it is moved from sunlight to shade, from daylight to incandescent light to fluorescent light, and, if possible, to colored light. Observe the same object in bright moonlight. Then try to see its colors in the dimmest light by which you can still make out the form of the object. If you are observant, you will have to admit that although your mind tells you the object remains the color or colors you know it to be in daylight or artificial light, your eyes rarely see that color. Even in bright daylight the color will not be uniform. In some areas it will be shaded, perhaps almost to black; other areas may be highlighted to such an extent that they appear white; and reflections from some other object may give the hue a different cast. Even without performing this experiment, you know this happens. The question, depending on your own attitude toward scientific phenomena, is either "Why?" or "So what?"

The answer to "So what?" is easy. If you're planning to paint anything—even blank walls—you're going to have to deal with color phenomena, and if you want to paint pictures that have the slightest suggestion of realism, you will have to learn something about the effects of light on color and the things that happen when colors are mixed.

The answers to the "why's" of color phenomena are much more complicated. There isn't space in this book to go into more than a few of the basic facts that are known about the behavior of color and light as they affect the painter, but if you want to pursue the matter further, there are books you can refer to which deal with many phases of color.

Seeing Color

THE SPECTRUM

In high school physics you probably learned that when a beam of sunlight, or light from any other source, goes through anything that acts as a prism (a droplet of water for instance), the light is refracted, or bent, and broken up into waves of various lengths. The visible wavelengths are the colors of the spectrum (and also of the rainbow, which is a manifestation of the spectrum). Red, which has the longest wavelength, appears at the top of the spectrum, and the other colors grade almost imperceptibly through orange, yellow, green, and blue, to violet, which has the shortest wavelength, at the bottom. Of course there are also longer and shorter light waves, such as infrared and ultraviolet, but they are not visible to the naked eye.

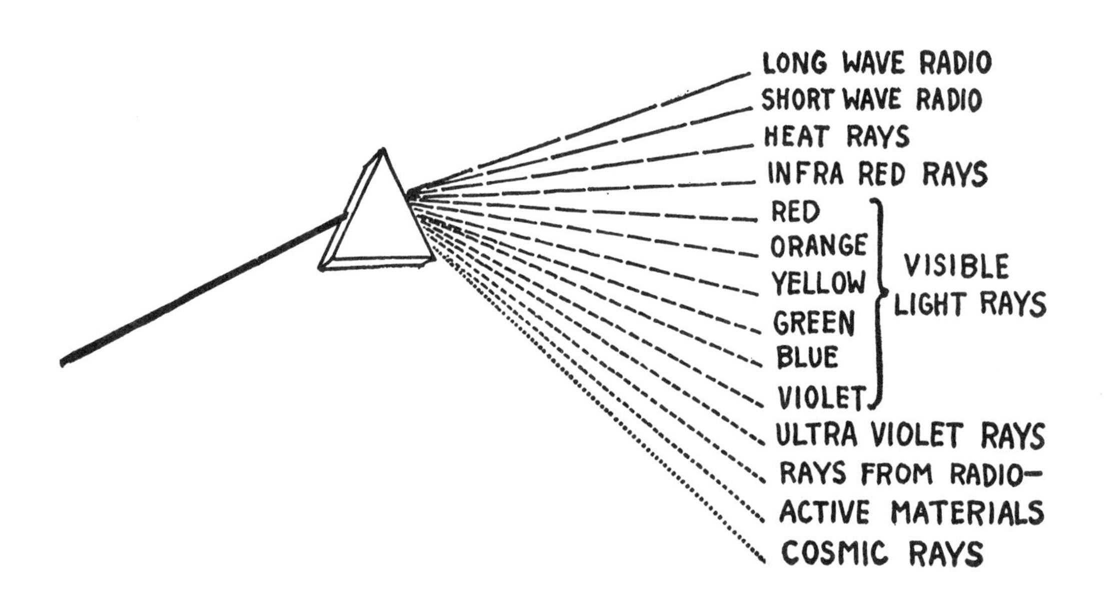

HOW YOU SEE COLORED OBJECTS

The surface of any object is seen by reflected light. If the surface is pure white, it will reflect all of the rays of the white light that reaches it and will therefore appear pure white. If the surface contains pigments, dyes, or other coloring agents, the light waves that correspond to the colors of the coloring agents will be reflected, but all other light waves will be absorbed. A red surface, for instance, will absorb the violet, blue, green, yellow, and orange light waves, but will reflect the red light waves, and will, therefore, appear red. A black surface will absorb all of the light waves, reflecting none. A black object is usually seen not by reflection, but by the absence of reflection and by comparison with surrounding objects.

This whole problem is complicated, of course, by many other factors—such as whether the surface is dull or shiny, and whether the light is bright or dim, direct or reflected. A glossy surface sometimes reflects so much light that it appears white at its points of maximum reflection, while a dull, matte surface of the same hue will appear much darker.

As already suggested, colored objects are not the same color in sunlight as in shadow, nor do they appear the same color on a gray day as on a bright sunny day. Nor will they seem the same indoors and out. Any woman who has tried to match colors knows that materials that appear to match, or at least to go well together, in a store with fluorescent lighting may not blend well at all when seen by daylight or even by incandescent light. Yet all of these lights are regarded as "ordinary" white light. The effects of colored lights are even more complicated, but they are usually of more concern to theatrical designers than to painters.

There are many other factors that affect the way we see—and can use—color that *are* important to painters. We'll get around to some of them after we learn a little about mixing color.

Mixing Color

Now that you know that color is the way we see light reflecting from surfaces containing coloring agents, or pigments, it is easier to understand that there are different sets of rules for mixing colored lights and for mixing pigments. Both sets of laws have to be taken into consideration in painting shadows and reflections on colored objects.

LIGHT MIXTURE

Light mixtures are called additive mixtures because when you mix colored light rays you are adding light to light, and when you add all the colors of the spectrum together, you get pure white light. Of course you don't need all of the colors of the spectrum for that. You can get white light by mixing the three light primaries. There's some question here as to which colors should be considered the light primaries. I see them as orange, green, and violet, which happen to be the pigment secondaries and which provide a very workable theory of color mixture for painters. However, some books on color describe the light primaries as red, green, and blue-violet, and in the theatre, where colored lights are standard equipment, they call them amber, cyanine, and magenta. Much of the difficulty stems from the inadequacy of our way of describing colors and the fact that in the spectrum one color grades so gradually into its neighbor that it's hard for the eye to judge where red becomes orange, green fades into blue, or blue into violet. So my orange may be your red, and what you think of as blue, I may call violet. Whatever names we give the light primaries, the full range of spectrum colors—as well as white light—can be produced by various combinations of two or more colors.

PIGMENT MIXTURE

The pigment primaries, as almost everyone learned in kindergarten or soon after, are red, yellow, and blue. In theory they combine to produce all other colors and when all mixed together should produce black. In fact it's a little different. Pigments are made from substances that aren't quite as pure or dependable in their behavior as colored lights. You can easily mix the pigment secondaries,

COLOR WHEELS

Some people find it easier to understand color relationships in terms of a color circle or color wheel. You can make your own with the pigments on your palette, adding intermediate hues between the primaries and secondaries.

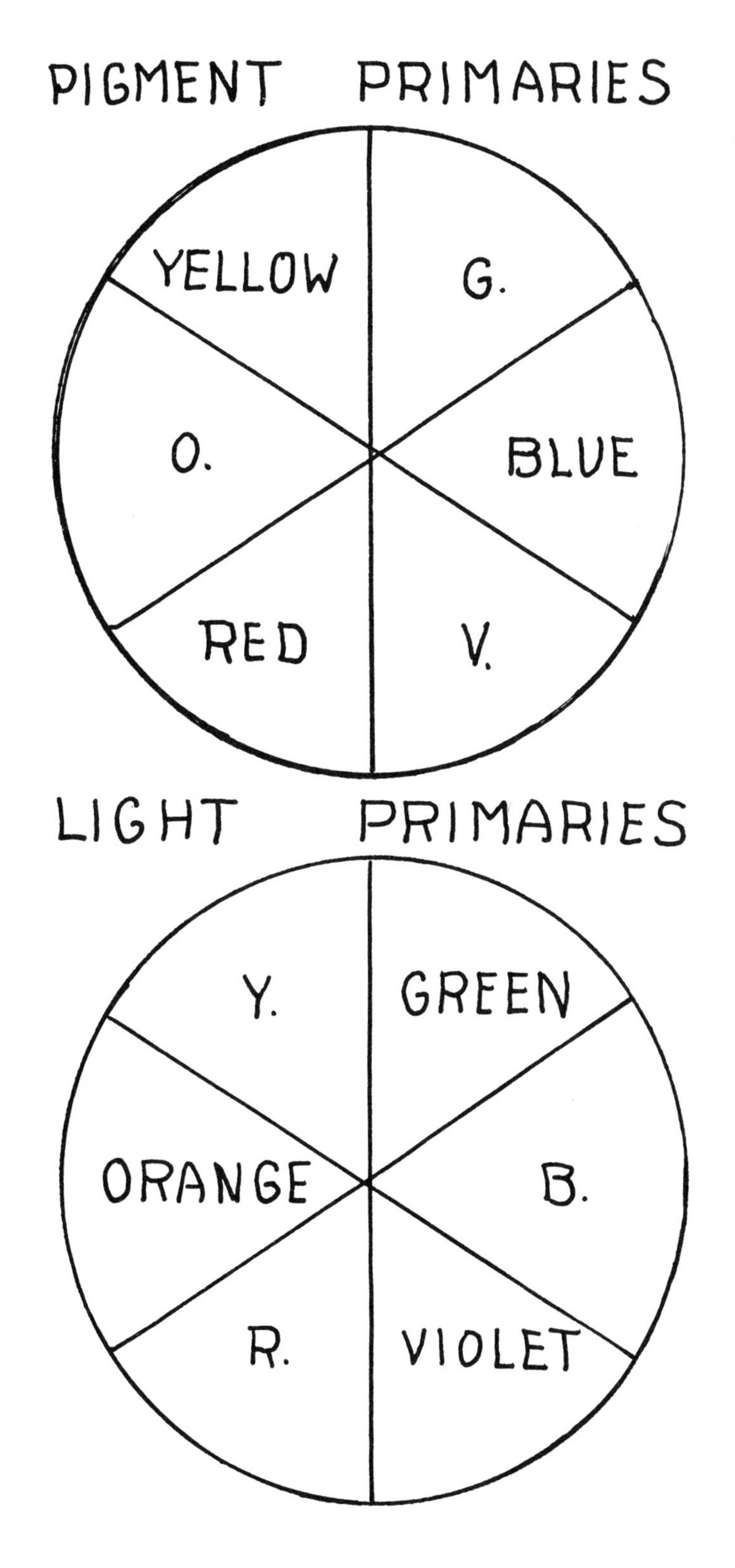

PIGMENT MIXTURE

Primaries are red, yellow, and blue. Secondaries are green, orange, and violet. Complementaries, which appear directly opposite each other on the color circle, are red and green, yellow and violet, and blue and orange.

LIGHT MIXTURE

Primaries are green, orange, and violet. Secondaries are red, yellow, and blue. Complementaries are the same as in pigment mixture.

FOUR RULES FOR MIXING COLOR BASED ON THE COLOR CIRCLE

1. Neighboring colors mix to make intermediaries.
2. Primaries mix to make secondaries.
3. Secondaries neutralize each other.
4. Complementaries neutralize each other.

orange, green, and violet, by combining, respectively, red and yellow, yellow and blue, and blue and red. However, the kind of orange, green, or violet you produce will depend on the characteristics of the red, yellow, or blue pigment used. Most bright red pigments tend slightly toward orange or blue, bright yellow pigments range from slightly greenish to slightly orange, and the strongest blues are likely to have a slight tinge of green or a slight undertone of violet. The secondaries mixed from such pigments will naturally vary considerably from pure green, orange, and violet. Since many different pigments are available under many different names, the only way you can ever learn what happens when you combine certain blues with certain yellows or reds is to mix them yourself and observe the differences. You'll find that not only are there significant differences in the range of colors produced, but that there are also interesting differences in brightness and dullness, transparency and opacity, and in texture.

You can experiment in any way you please, trying mixtures of as many colors as you can afford to buy. The following exercise suggests just one way to go about it.

Clip a half sheet of rough watercolor paper to a cardboard or drawing board. Squeeze out a good-sized dollop of each of your pigments, arranging them roughly in the order of the spectrum. First paint a series of strokes across the top of the sheet with each of your reds, next to them a series of yellows, then a series of blues. Beneath this row of pure colors experiment with secondary mixtures. See how many different greens, oranges, and violets you can produce. If your palette includes—as it should—a green, an orange, and a violet, paint comparison swatches of each unmixed secondary near the ones produced by mixing primaries.

Now try a series of intermediate hues: red-orange, yellow-orange, yellow-green, blue-green, blue-violet, and red-violet. Each intermediate is a combination of a primary and one of the secondaries adjacent to it in the spectrum. Actually a wide variety of hues can be mixed in each intermediate band, ranging from the almost pure primary to the almost pure secondary.

After you have experimented with your bright colors, fill a sheet with grayed or neutralized colors. First paint swatches of all your pigment neutrals—brownish reds, umbers, grays, black. Then try mixing neutrals with each of your bright pigments.

COMPLEMENTARY COLORS

As mentioned before, mixtures that include equal amounts of the three pigment primaries, red, yellow, and blue, are supposed to produce black. Actually, the best you can get with pigment mixtures is usually a gray-brown, but any mixture that includes even a small proportion of the third primary will tend to be at least slightly grayed. While experimenting with the mixture of intermediate colors, you undoubtedly found that some combinations of primary and secondary produced neutral colors rather than bright intermediates. What you were discovering was the neutralizing effect of complementary mixture.

Each primary has as its complement the secondary formed by the other two primaries. Thus, green (yellow mixed with blue) is the complement of red; orange (yellow and red) is the complement of blue; and violet (blue and red) is the complement of yellow. Complementary relationships also exist between intermediate hues. Blue-green is the complement of red-orange, for example.

Any mixture of complementary colors includes all three primaries and is, therefore, bound to be somewhat grayed. The degree of neutralization will depend on the proportion of each color used. The brilliance of a color can be toned down by adding just a small amount of its complement. Theoretically, an equal mixture of complementary colors should result in a neutral gray. Grayed tones can also be produced by mixing secondaries, since any two secondaries include the three primaries.

Experiment with mixtures of complementaries and secondaries until you can produce a wide range of neutralized colors.

THE THREE DIMENSIONS OF COLOR

Many artists find it helpful to think of every color as having three dimensions: hue, saturation, and value. Hue is what we think of as the name of the color—red, yellow, blue, etc. Saturation, or intensity, is its strength or brightness. A clear bright red is highly saturated; a brownish or grayish red is dull and has a low degree of saturation. Value is the lightness or darkness of the color. Pink is a light value of red, burgundy a dark one. Any hue may be represented in a full range of values and degrees of saturation.

You may find it useful to make graded value and saturation charts for each of the pigments on your palette.

SEEING AND PAINTING SHADOWS ON COLORED SURFACES

The diagram below, based on the rules of light and pigment mixture given on page 41, shows how colored objects are affected by three different kinds of light. In each case, the left side of the cube is seen in bright (white) sunlight and is what we would call the normal color of the surface. The shaded side is affected by color reflections from the blue sky, while the shadowed underside is affected by reflections from the orange earth. The color of each shadow area is a mixture of the local color of the object and the direct or reflected light it receives. Obviously this example is based on a specific combination of circumstances. In painting shadows you must deal with whatever combination of lighting and reflections you see or invent. Remember that when you look at nature you are seeing it in terms of the light primaries, but when you mix paint you do it in terms of the pigment primaries.

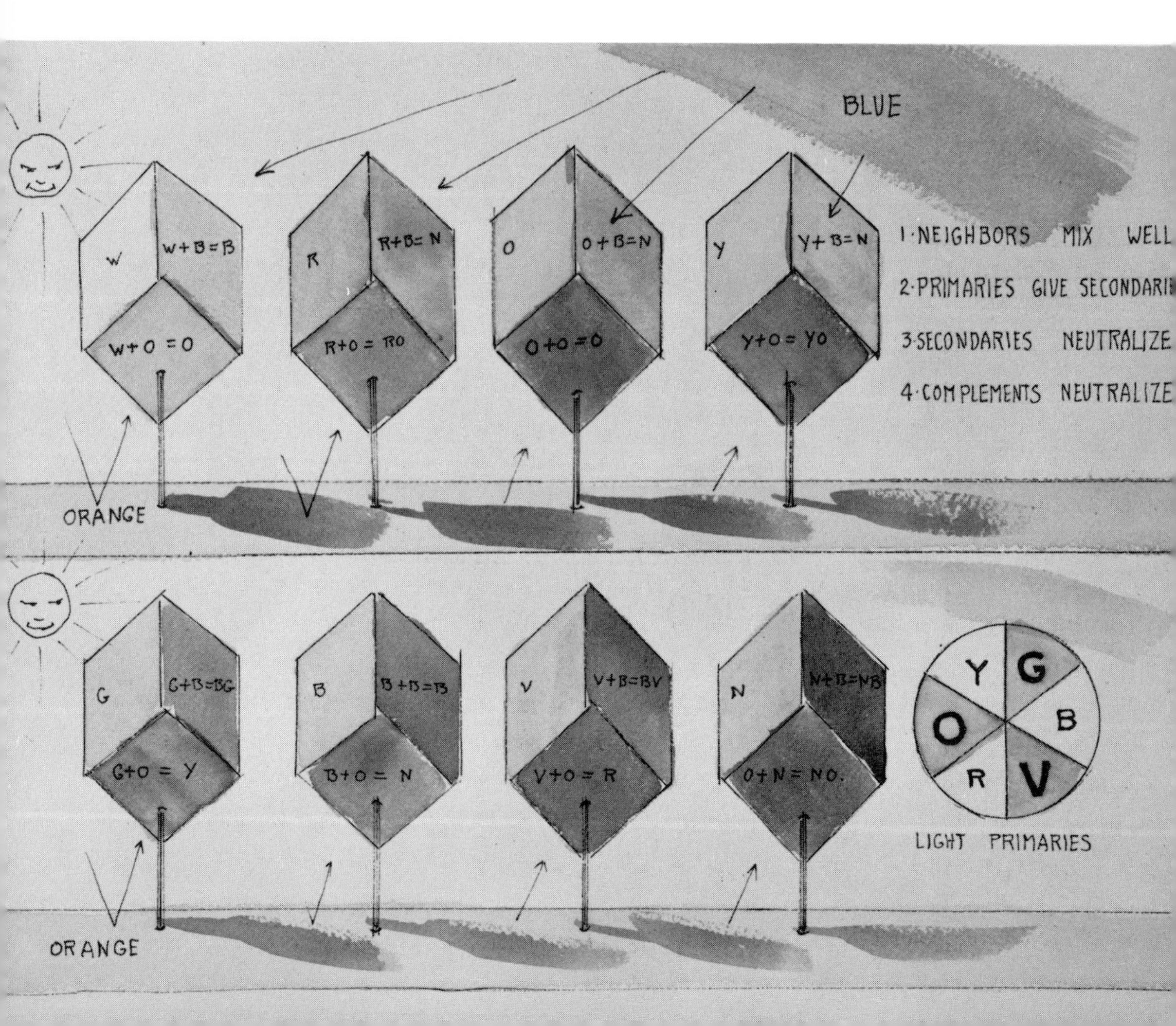

Using Color

PAINTING A PICTURE

When you have had your fill of abstract brushmarks, black-and-white pictures, and playing with color mixing, you can put them all together and paint a picture in color. Eventually you can paint in whatever style you please, but to begin with you had better start with old-fashioned academic realism. Most of the famous masters of modern art started that way—so you will be in good company. You may even like it, and you will still be in good company.

For your first picture practically any landscape should be noncommittal enough to permit you to practice technique without getting tangled up in any of the more complex ideas you will have to wrestle with later. Don't even think about "isms." Simply become a color camera and reproduce exactly what you see, changing nature only enough to omit nonessential details and to place things in the most interesting way possible on the paper.

I have decided to do the Joe Doaks house on Main Street. You know the place, a wooden house with grass in front, which Mr. Doaks mows every Sunday. There is a wall, a tree, and a fence of some kind in front of it. Mrs. Doaks keeps all the shades exactly at half-mast during the day. The house is usually painted white, sometimes gray or yellow, and it has green blinds. In other words, it is a typical suburban American home. I suggest you choose a Joe Doaks house near you and use it over and over again, painting it in different mannerisms as we go through them.

Now before you begin to paint the subject, you must first consider its color in terms of what you have already learned. The hues of the major color areas will be readily apparent, and it should not be too difficult to distinguish between bright and dull colors. So let's concentrate on values first. How light or dark is the subject? It may help you to number the values, using #1 as the lightest and #10 for the darkest. This is not to be confused with number painting! It simply eliminates the difficulty of keeping track of the natural changes of light that occur in any landscape during a lapse of time. The sun and the shadows cast by it will not, unfortunately, stay where they were when you blocked in your picture. In fact,

The Joe Doaks House

This is my version of the Joe Doaks house described in the text. Although somewhat simplified, it's a straightforward reproduction of nature. As we go along, we will try other approaches to painting it.

the sun may have flitted off completely by the time you have unpacked your watercolor kit and are ready to paint.

As an aid to judging values, use a black card with two ¼-inch holes cut in it (such as was shown on page 34). Hold the card at arm's length, keeping your elbows straight, so that with one eye closed and the other peering through the holes you can compare a spot of porch roof with one of tree or lawn.

Once you have numbered the values of your color areas, you are ready to paint them. An ox-hair brush, one inch or larger, is a good tool for this job. The lightest value, #1, may be left white since the white paper is the lightest value you can get.

Now, dip the brush into the desired color and move it sideways on the palette a few times in order to avoid getting chunks of paint on your paper. Start right now forming the habit of pinching your brush between your thumb and index finger rather than slapping it on a sponge or rag. This way you will eventually learn just how wet or dry your brush is by feeling it. The other way only the sponge or rag will ever know, and that will never be of much help to you. Remember to dip into your water jar to rinse out the last color used before starting on a new area using a different one.

My house had a red roof so I dipped up Cadmium Red Light with a medium-wet brush and painted the roof with it—although I modified the color before it had dried. For the grass (value #2) I again used a medium-wet brush, this time with Cadmium Yellow Medium and a mere suggestion of Phthalocyanine Green. This may remind you of an old-fashioned cookbook—a pinch of this and a dab of that—but there is no way of giving you a formula for how much color. You simply have to try, yourself. If it comes out right, fine; if it comes out wrong, say whatever you say when you're really mad and try again. Remember, though, watercolor fades as it dries. Make allowances for that.

To paint the sky (values #2, #3, and #4) I first wet the whole sky area with water to fill the pores of the paper and to prevent staining, then used a very wet brush loaded with Phthalocyanine Blue. I find it easier to paint an area of this size upside down. However, you can paint it at any angle that gives you the freest movement of hand and arm.

For the darker foliage and the shadow on the lawn I used a brushful of Cadmium Orange and Raw Umber with a little green added. I put in the lawn shadow while the rest of the painting was still wet, but waited until the sky had dried before rough brushing the leafy edges of the top of the tree. Incidentally, this picture gave me a chance to paint three kinds of edges between colors. The edge of the lawn and the lower part of the tree are wet blended (wet into wet). There are hard edges along the ridgepole and the edge of the porch roof (wet onto dry), and the edge of the treetops are rough brushed. For the rough-brushed edges, the lighter color was allowed to dry, then a dry, flatly held brush smeared rather than painted the leafy area.

Be sure to paint your own version of the Joe Doaks house, not mine. These step-by-step directions are meant only as a guide, not as a set of rules to be followed. Finish off the rest of the painting on your own. When you get to the windows, though, avoid uniform blue rectangles. Windows will sometimes reflect trees or sky, but otherwise they generally appear warm and dark.

El Cid, Balboa Park, San Diego BY ELIOT O'HARA

Selective color can be applied in abstract patterns for purposes of design rather than realism. The picture may be completely abstract or—as here—abstract color can be combined with calligraphic line to suggest a recognizable scene.

SELECTIVE COLOR

There are three approaches to color for the painter. One is the imitation of nature—no easy task, but by some application it can be mastered. The picture we just painted of the Joe Doaks house is based on what we actually saw—or might have seen. It is imitative color. The second approach is based on mood or feeling. Although the effect may be realistic, the color is used to express emotion. This is expressionistic color. The third is an arbitrary use of whatever colors you choose. I call this selective color. It is a first step toward abstraction. The use of selective color requires the same kind of taste and the sense of design that works in choosing your clothes or the upholstery, rugs, and draperies for your living room.

Using your own picture of the Joe Doaks house as a starting point, you are ready to experiment with selective color. Be sure that the painting you use is your own work. Do not refer to my illustration of the Doaks house or to another painting by someone else. You must be adamant about not copying others or paraphrasing their ideas in paint. My version of the Doaks house is reproduced in black and white to force you to use your own color.

Now, as you start mixing paint, forget about what your picture represents. You are like a composer sitting at his piano, searching for chords that will sound right. He tries combinations and discards or accepts them according to his personal choice.

Since there must be a starting point, why not begin with the color of the roof and the color of the grass in sunlight? Try variations of both of these colors clockwise and counterclockwise around the color wheel until you find the hues that satisfy you. Make them lighter or darker, brighter or grayer. Keep trying until you have something that suits you better than the colors of Joe's roof and lawn. Since you are an artist, you should have better taste in color than Joe. Don't be too easily satisfied. Keep working until you have tried a lot of combinations. Use a third color if you wish, or more. Use the bright colors, or neutralize them as far as complete gray. As in music, the pure colors are clear, like the notes of a flute, while the neutrals have overtones like those of an oboe or a bassoon. It is up to you to decide whether you will have muted colors or clear colors, or combinations of both. They do not have to be the colors of nature at all. Remember the strangely colored faces in the paintings of the Norwegian artist Edvard Munch, or the bright green face of a Van Gogh self-portrait?

Like a composer putting together an orchestral work, you have many choices. For his high and low, you have light and dark. For his octave, you have the spectrum. For his overtones, you have contrasts of intensity and neutralization, and a multitude of surface textures at your disposal. As he does, you may choose your key, devise an accompaniment, use minor or major, or deal in dissonance. Your object is to select and orchestrate color rather than to make a likeness of the house. As in any work of art, you should use restraint. The employment of too many colors without control is like sitting on the keyboard of the piano.

Remember, for this exercise you are choosing colors with only one question in mind, "Do they go well together?" You are in a realm where there is no good or bad. The only thing that matters is whether you yourself accept or reject the final result.

Palm Patterns, reproduced on page 99, was painted in this way. The fronds, for instance, were painted orange instead of the yellow-green of the actual scene.

Lonely Beach BY ELIOT O'HARA

Neutralized tones of orange, blue, and violet suggest the shifting colors of sunset at the shore. Small touches of bright, strong color focus attention on the tiny figure and emphasize the loneliness of the scene.

KEYED COLOR

Everything in life is seen only in relation to its surroundings. A giant in a community of pygmies may be a dwarf in a community of giants. In the same way, every color in a painting is seen in relation to surrounding colors and may appear to change hue, value, and intensity as neighboring colors are introduced. Light values will appear lighter against dark values, and dark values will be darker against light values. Bright colors will appear brighter against dark, or dull, or complementary colors. These are the basic rules for keying color and many artists use them—whether consciously or not—whenever they paint.

The use of keyed color can mean the difference between a successful and an unsuccessful painting. I once watched a fellow artist do a portrait of a young Negro girl, which I thought was very good in every respect except color. To me, the face appeared to have a sickly green pallor. Months later, when I saw the same picture in a watercolor show, the green cast was gone and the face looked warm and healthy, yet the only thing actually changed was the background. Instead of the pale pink boudoir of the original scene, the artist had substituted green palmetto fronds with sunlight streaming through them. The complementary pink background had emphasized the green tones in the skin, but the green and gold background toned down the green and brought out the warmer skin tones.

As an exercise in keying color, do two pictures which are alike in subject, size, and areas. Use the same color for the main color area in each picture, but alter the surrounding colors so that the main color appears lighter and more neutral in one, darker and more intense in the other.

LIMITED HUES

Many interesting paintings have been done with extremely limited palettes. As an exercise in color restraint, paint a picture in which all the warm colors are suggested by one warm neutral like Burnt Umber and all the cool colors by one cool neutral, Payne's Gray perhaps. Try other combinations in which you use a wider variety of neutrals. Then try some in which a note or two of bright color is added as an accent.

DOMINANT COLOR

Most paintings have a dominant color tone. Although all the colors of the spectrum may be visible in the picture, one or two colors seem to predominate and to set the mood. Many painters tend to do this subconsciously. However, you may find it useful to experiment with the use of a dominant color to suggest mood.

Paint several pictures of the same subject—the Joe Doaks house again if you wish—in which all of the colors used are falsified slightly in the direction of one particular hue. The picture should have somewhat the effect of a monochrome. Although all of the colors on your palette may be used in the painting, many of them will be neutralized to such an extent that the final result will have an overall tone of blue, or green, or orange, or whatever color you have decided to make the dominant one.

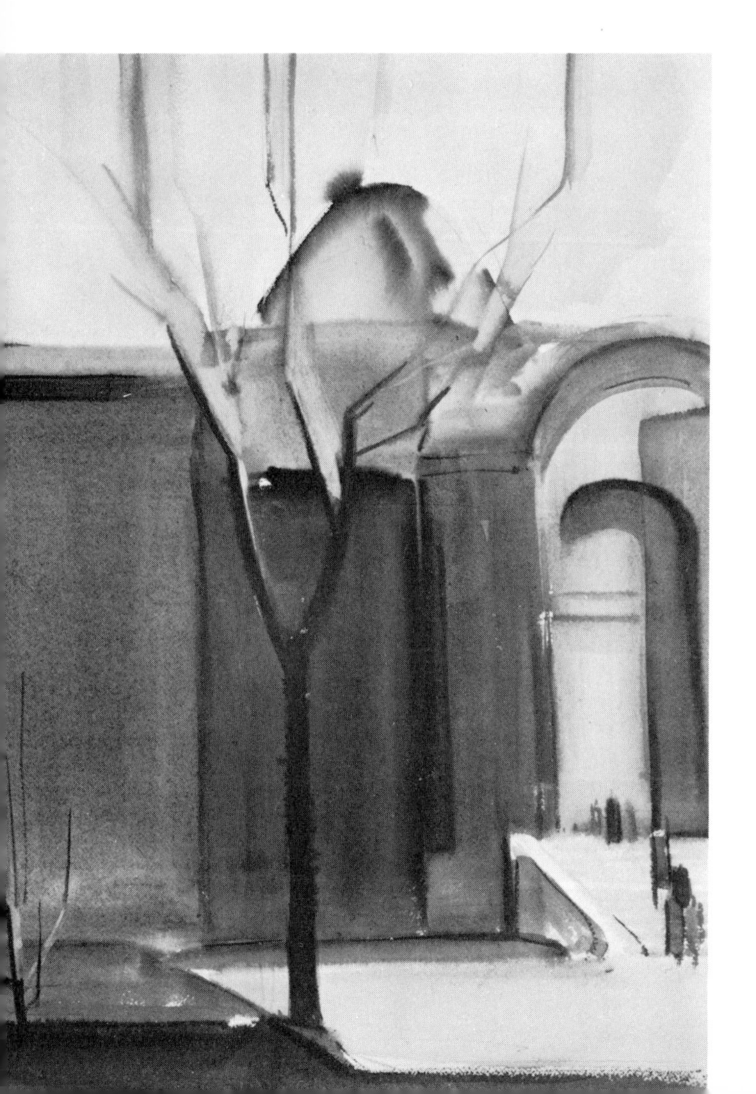

Portal

BY ELIOT O'HARA

An almost monochromatic color scheme dramatizes the simple linear pattern of the tree.

Nightfall, Santa Barbara BY ELIOT O'HARA

COLLECTION OF PHILADELPHIA WATER COLOR CLUB

To convey a mood of quiet stillness, I used a very limited palette for this picture and allowed green, black, and violet to dominate it.

In doing this exercise, you may find that you dislike many of the effects produced. Some of them will seem flat, drab, weak, and amateurish. That should deter you from making such mistakes unintentionally in future work. On the other hand, some of the paintings will appear stronger than you expect them to, with startling suggestions of mood or emotional content. You might keep them in mind for future use.

After you have tried a dozen or so extreme variations, paint the scene again as you would like to see it. This time use color to express what you want to say about the subject. Use everything you have learned about color so far to emphasize important areas, to tone down lesser areas, or to establish whatever color mood or color key you wish.

Cadiz Cathedral BY ELIOT O'HARA

Light and Shadow

IF MOST of the paintings you have done so far—whether they were done as experiments or were intended as finished paintings—have seemed flat and lacking in three-dimensional form, you probably need to pay more attention to the way light and shadow define form.

One of the best ways to study the effects of light and shadow on a variety of shapes is to set up a still life composed of objects with definite geometric shapes, such as a ball, a cube, a cylinder, and a cone. If you have a lamp that throws a fairly strong directional light and that can be moved easily, set the lamp in various positions in relation to the still-life setup and study the effects you see. Then paint the same setup—or a similar one—in ordinary daylight indoors and in bright sunlight outdoors. Make simple pencil studies of the shadow patterns with the light source in different locations and at different intensities.

When the light source is bright—as on a very sunny day—and from a definite direction, the contrasts between lighted areas and shadowed areas will be strong, and the objects will cast their shadows away from the light source. On a day when the sky is bright but overcast, the lighting will be flat as it will also be if a room is flooded with indirect artificial light. In such cases, there may be no shadows at all. However, if a secondary light source is introduced—such as a flood lamp or a stray beam of sunlight peeping through the overcast—there may be very soft, diffused shadows.

In making your studies, pay particular attention to the location of the shadows in relation to the light source (or sources, if there is more than one), and the differences in values of the shadows in different locations. Notice the way a shadow area is affected by

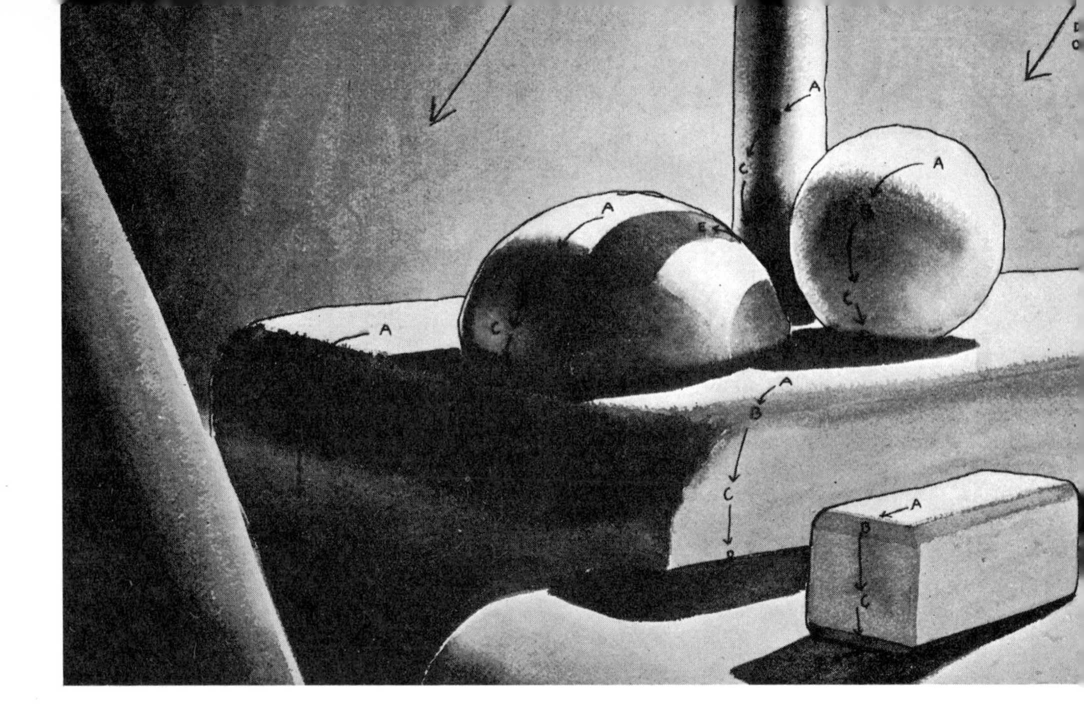

Any still-life setup can be used to study the way light and shadow describe form. In this sketch, A indicates brightly lighted areas; B, shaded areas that receive indirect sunlight; C, shaded areas lightened by bright reflections; D, black edges beneath objects; and E, cast shadows.

the shape of the object that casts the shadow, and by the shape of the object on which the shadow falls. Distinguish between cast shadows and shadowed areas that are not in the direct path of the light, and notice the way brightly lighted areas reflect light into nearby shadow areas.

As the illustration of the still life indicates, there are five kinds of lighting to watch for:

A. Areas that receive the direct light of the sun or other light source. They are brightly lighted.

B. Shaded areas that receive indirect sunlight or lamplight. These areas vary in their degree of brightness or shadow, depending on their position in relation to the light source. Some sections may be only a few degrees darker than the brightest areas, others may be almost as dark as the darkest cast shadows.

C. Shaded areas that receive reflections from illuminated surfaces nearby. These areas will be lightened by the bright reflections.

Los Arcos, Taxco BY ELIOT O'HARA

COURTESY TOLEDO MUSEUM OF ART

The same principles of light and shadow shown in the still-life diagram apply in this pattern of architectural forms seen by moonlight.

D. Black edges beneath objects. These are very dark shadows that appear where overhanging edges prevent light from reaching crevices between or beneath them. They create strong outlines and can be very useful in defining forms.

E. Cast shadows, or shadows that are created when one object blocks the light and prevents it from falling directly on another object. If it falls on a flat surface, the cast shadow assumes a shape similar to that of the object that throws it. Otherwise, the shadow adapts itself to the contours of the surface it falls on. In either case, the shape of the shadow will be distorted by the angle of the light source. If it is low, as the sun is in the early morning and late afternoon, the shadows will be elongated. If it is high, as the sun is in the late morning and early afternoon, the shadows will be foreshortened. If all this sounds pretty obvious, you would be surprised how easy it is to forget the obvious when you have a lot of new problems to work out. The depth of value of the cast shadow depends on the intensity of the light source and other factors. Shadows usually appear much darker on a bright clear day, for example, than on a bright but hazy day.

Corrections

JUST AS it is good training to attend drawing classes without an eraser, it is good training in watercolor painting to think of mistakes as impossible to correct and of spoiled watercolors as irretrievable. Most of them are. However, there *are* ways to correct some mistakes. Obviously it is better to paint a good watercolor to begin with than to try to repair a bad one, but here are some "gimmicks" that may help to retrieve an occasional picture. The chances are 50-50 that you will spoil the picture completely, but if it's already a mess, what can you lose by trying? One word of warning: Don't stop to fiddle with minor inaccuracies while you're painting the picture. Get it finished while the impulse is still fresh. Then, if you think it needs reworking, you can try one of the following procedures.

Erasing Construction Lines

If you covered construction lines with dark or relatively opaque pigment, you probably won't see them in the finished painting. However, they can be very annoying if they show through lighter, more transparent pigments. Light lines (made with a 4B pencil) can usually be removed with an art gum eraser. Colors made from dyes probably won't be disturbed at all, but colors composed of pigment particles might be loosened by erasure. Keep the problem in mind and decide whether it's worth the risk.

Lightening and Removing Color

There are various ways of lightening color passages after a painting is dry, and it is even possible to remove color completely

To add white cloud masses to this picture after the sky wash had dried, I brushed the cloud areas with a bristle brush filled with clear water, then blotted the loosened paint with a dry cloth. The longer the interval between wetting and wiping, the more color can be removed.

from fairly large areas. Naturally, dyes, or staining colors, will be harder to remove completely than pigment colors and some papers will take more abuse than others. Also, some papers will respond to one treatment but not to another. Here are some of the procedures:

1. You can lighten colors in a limited area by careful erasing with a soft eraser. Beware, however, of attempting to lighten large areas by this method because it is difficult to do it evenly.

2. An ink eraser, or gum with an abrasive in it, will remove most of the color from the tops of the ridges of a rough paper, but will leave color in the valleys. This will give a speckled effect, which is fine if that's what you want. If it's not, don't use this method. Sandpaper can be used in the same way.

3. Colors may also be lightened by careful scrubbing with an oil painter's bristle brush and water. Be prepared to blot up the loosened paint with a clean soft cloth. Although this method will leave an even surface, it may also leave a dark line around the edge of the treated area.

4. To remove color completely from large areas of any hot-pressed, or smooth, paper and from most rough papers (the surfaces of Fabriano and D'Arches papers, however, are too soft for this method), brush the area to be treated with your watercolor brush filled with plain water. Let this sit for a few minutes, but don't let any part of the repair area dry and don't let any other part of the picture get wet. Soak up excess water with blotting paper or a dry cloth until the paper is merely damp, and rub briskly across the entire repair area and adjacent parts with a dry cloth. Then, quickly, before the paper dries any more, use the art gum eraser to remove the color. The dampened area should come clean without disturbing the thoroughly dry parts surrounding it. The result should be pure white paper unless some part of the dampened area dried too soon.

5. You can remove the darkest colors with a sponge. However, the area that has been sponged may have a ragged edge, and it will be gray, not pure white. Unless it can be painted over crisply, the effect will be bad. If you use a sponge, be sure to have a clean dry cloth in your left hand to wipe the paper dry as the color becomes loosened by the sponging.

6. It is possible to outline a small area with a sharp knife, then peel off the top layer of paper with the knife point. However, in this case, the resulting white spot cannot be repainted.

Adding White Highlights

White highlights should be planned at the beginning of the painting and areas that are to be pure white paper should be left unpainted. However, if a spot that was supposed to be a highlight is accidentally covered with color, you can easily pick out the color with a penknife or razor blade by making a V-shaped cut or surface scratch. A knife can also be used to trim up a bad dark edge against a lighter ground.

Chinese White, an opaque white, is also useful for adding white highlights. Although some purists frown on its use in watercolor, it is now generally accepted, as long as it is not used in excess or mixed with other colors. If it is used that way, the medium is no longer watercolor but gouache—which is all right if you want to paint gouaches. There is more information on gouache and other related mediums in another chapter.

Advanced Watercolor Techniques

ONCE YOU have gained sufficient control of watercolor on rough paper to turn out realistic reproductions of landscapes, still lifes, and other subjects, you should be ready to tackle more advanced problems. Although the techniques suggested in this section are not for absolute novices, don't put off trying them for too long. It may take a lot of practice to gain mastery of wet blending, for instance, but you'll never do it if you don't get started. Or you may think that you really don't care particularly for calligraphy, or unpainted intervals, or working on smooth paper, and decide to ignore them. You can if you want to, but try them first before you make up your mind. You might discover something in them you didn't know was there—perhaps a way of working that suits you.

Transitions—Gradation in Nature and in Painting

Since the mind very easily deceives the eye, you should become aware as early as possible of transitions in fields of color such as the sky or a still-life background or a table top. Because you know the sky is blue or the table top green-gray, you will tend to paint them so, uniformly. However, large areas of color are rarely uniform in value or hue. The sky on a cloudless day or on a completely foggy or dull day varies so imperceptibly that you will have to look carefully to see the gradations.

If you are painting outdoors on a warm, sunny, cloudless day, lie on your back for a time and really look at the sky. You will discover it is quite different from the uniform tint with which most artists would cover their paper. They look quizzically at the sky, say knowingly, "Yes, cobalt with a little green," and brush it on without another thought.

If you study it more carefully, you will see that the sky actually varies from light at one point to darker at another, and the dark part may not be the same hue or saturation as the lighter one. Or the sky may differ in value from horizon to zenith, and in hue from left to right.

Goat Island Light BY ELIOT O'HARA

Wet-blended edges and soft transitions suggest the enveloping mistiness of coastal fog.

It is easy to establish the truth of this. Hold two small mirrors at angles that reflect widely separated bits of sky. Or, as you did in checking values, punch two holes about three inches apart in a card or sheet of paper. Hold the card about six inches from your face and look with one eye from one hole to the other. However you hold the card, the two samples of sky will probably never quite match. In fact, they may often seem completely unrelated.

Once you have really seen these variations or transitions in the sky, look for them in other elements of the scene. Then paint your picture with awareness of all the gradual changes that are taking place within it.

As an example of what to look for, let us assume that you are painting on a clear day and that the sun is on your left. This will mean that the sky on the left side of the picture will be warmer and lighter than on the right, and, if the sun is not too high above the horizon, less saturated and lighter in value than the highest part of the sky. The shading of the grass in the same scene, however, may be reversed. If you look at the grass on your left, you will be looking at the shadow side of the blades so the lawn will appear darker on the left than on the right where you see the sunlit sides. The darker-colored grass on the left may appear warmer if the sun shines through it, but cooler if your angle of vision is such that you see the cast shadows.

Now, with a sky grading from light to dark and a field of grass grading from dark to light, add an area of water with reflections in it. Close by, you will see surfaces reflected in the far side of the ripples as well as the near side and there will be some refraction into the underwater color. In the distance you will see only the near side of the ripples and the angle will make them reflect the sky. Thus, the transitions in a sky reflected in water are not merely the reverse of those in the sky itself but are conditioned by other factors.

The colors and values of all other elements in the scene—earth, roofs, walls, etc.—will have varying textures, and parts will be seen in different kinds of light and shadow. None of them will appear uniform in color or value.

Look back over some of your older pictures for one that was painted in even flat tones. Do it over now with emphasis on transitions within each area. Exaggerate the transitions rather than level them. You will be surprised at the new vitality in your painting.

Wet-Blended Edges for Soft Transitions

The edges between colors and values in a watercolor can be hard, soft, or some combination or variation of the two. Some painters prefer one or the other and develop it into a personal style or mannerism. Most painters use all types of edges from time to time.

Hard edges, like the black lines in stained-glass designs or in the paintings of Rouault, tend to divide the picture into a series of definite sensations or compartments. Blurred edges, on the other hand, provide soft transitions, allowing the viewer's eye to move gradually from one area to another. Blurred edges are especially useful where a vague, misty quality is wanted.

As an exercise in this technique, paint several watercolors in which you try to avoid making any hard or sharp edges at all. This will be difficult and you may not succeed with the first few. In order to keep the edges soft, you will have to keep the paper wet, and each edge must be blended out to pure white or must have another wet brushful set down adjacent to it before it can dry.

Begin by sketching the outline you want in pencil. Then wet the paper all over and start to work in one of the upper corners. After putting in the first few colors, you can blend them into pure water and then carry the water across the paper again. Tipping the paper toward you helps you to keep it wet.

Coastal Fog BY ELIOT O'HARA

The soft, wet-blended edges of the fog contrast with the hard edges of rock and water not yet enveloped in the mist.

Ebbing Tide BY ELIOT O'HARA

COURTESY OF THE MONTCLAIR ART MUSEUM, NEW JERSEY

Maine Anchorage BY ELIOT O'HARA

Desert Sand BY ELIOT O'HARA

In this painting of sand dunes in Death Valley there are many delicate gradations of tone produced by wet blending. Those in the sky can be seen even in black and white, but the subtle gradations in the dunes are almost lost in reproduction. Hard edges define the mountains against the sky and the dunes against the mountains. Combinations of rough and smooth brushing describe the foreground.

It is usually better to complete the work on each small area before going on to the next. If you jump about the paper doing the light values first or doing similar colors at the same time, these isolated spots are likely to dry, making it hard to maintain the soft edge. If you do have to leave an area to dry, fade it out to pure water. Then, when you come back to it, you can wet the soft edge again and blend in the new adjacent area.

If you are a slow worker, you may end up with unwanted hard edges in spite of all your care. The only way I've discovered to hide them is to wet the area evenly so that the paper is damp but not wet. Then, using very little water, fuse the edge with some of the darker of the two adjoining colors. Be careful not to brush or rub the paper too much or you may loosen the paint on the surrounding dampened surface.

Working on Smooth Paper

It is far more difficult to control the flow of water on the smooth-surfaced watercolor papers than on the grainy surfaces of the rough papers. However, although smooth paper is harder to work with, it has certain compensating advantages. Colors appear more brilliant and more subtle in their gradations than on rough-surfaced papers where the grain tends to break up the color, giving it a slightly stippled, grayed appearance. There are also certain technical tricks that will work much better on smooth paper than on rough. And of course you can make longer strokes before your brush needs replenishing. Some contemporary painters prefer smooth or semi-smooth papers for most of their work and many others use it for certain kinds of subjects. Gertrude Schweitzer, whose *Girl in Red Dress* is reproduced on page 70, often works on smooth or semi-smooth papers. The late Charles H. Woodbury liked to use smooth papers for subjects such as *Sunken Ledges,* on page 106, which required delicate gradations of color.

In painting on smooth paper, the paint forms a thin layer that dries more quickly than the tiny pools of color formed on the grainy surface of rough paper. Therefore, speed is even more essential if you want to put an even wash on the paper. If you use a normally wet brush, a slow-drying drop or ridge of wet paint will collect quickly at the lowest point of the painted area. To avoid this, use a dryer brush than you are used to and cover each area quickly. When a drop or ridge does form, it should be picked up before it dries. However, it can also be moved around on previously dampened surrounding areas by tipping the paper. Some painters become quite skillful at herding pools of very wet paint into controlled results by tilting their papers.

You will also find that it is harder to produce ragged edges and broken color on smooth paper. You can still use rough-brushed strokes, but the effect will not be as ragged as on rough paper. However, there are other interesting tricks and textural effects that you can try on smooth paper that would never work on rough paper. To produce a soft edge, for instance, wet an almost dry

Wax-Resistant Lines

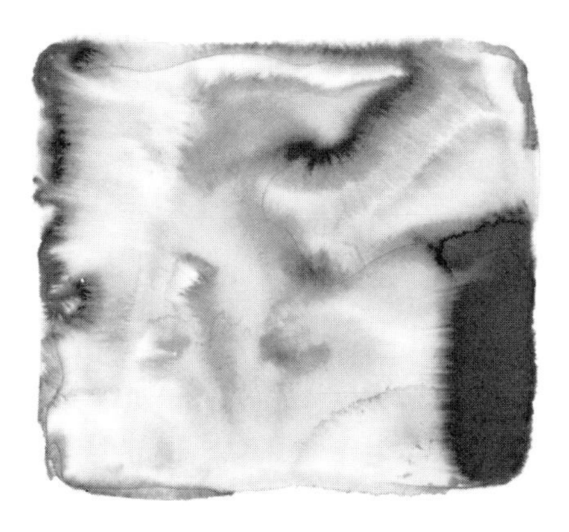

Mingled Colors

India Ink and Watercolor Wash

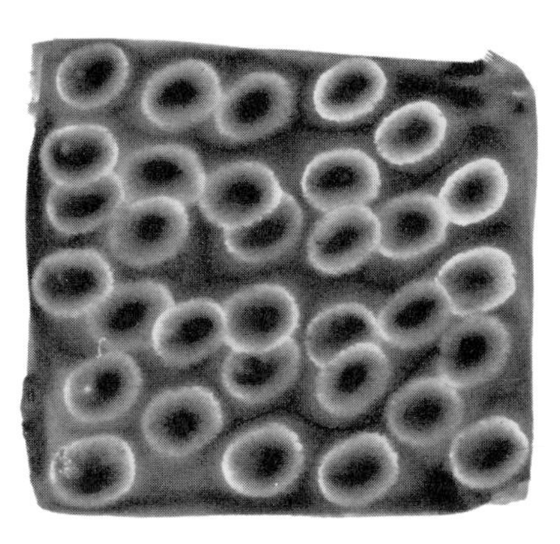

Fingerprints in Wet Wash

Salt Textures

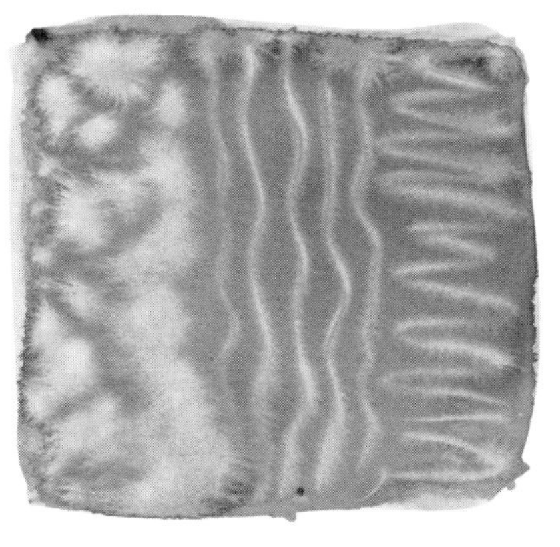

Oozles

Girl in Red Dress BY GERTRUDE SCHWEITZER

COURTESY BOWDOIN COLLEGE MUSEUM OF ART, BRUNSWICK, MAINE

In painting this watercolor portrait on semi-smooth paper the artist maintained expert control by tilting her paper to herd the wet flowing colors exactly where she wanted them to go.

area slightly and with a clean, dry brush remove nearly all of the color, leaving a soft edge instead of a hard one.

Here are a few more tricks to try. You may find others yourself.

MINGLED COLORS

Wet the paper, then dip the brush, damp but not wet, into two different colors, one light and one dark. Don't mix the colors on your palette. Let them run together on the paper.

WAX-RESISTANT AREAS

Make wax marks or lines on the paper, using an ordinary child's crayon, then paint over the area. The waxy area will resist the watercolor paint but will add its own interesting color and texture. Wax lines or areas can also be added by placing a piece of wax paper over the watercolor paper and transferring the wax to the watercolor paper by applying pressure. A dull-edged knife, for example, or a pencil can be used to draw rather fine wax lines. A painting in which this technique was used is shown on page 158.

INDIA INK

Using a pen or a very fine brush, draw lines on smooth watercolor paper with India ink. Before the ink is dry, paint the areas adjacent to the lines with clear water. Such effects can be very useful at times.

FINGER MARKS

Paint a large area with a fairly deep tone. While the paint is still wet, use your fingers to make a variety of marks.

OOZLES

Cover a large area with a wash of any color. Then, with a brush filled with clear water, drip water drops into the partly dried wash and draw lines through the wash. Oozles were used to suggest shifting sand in the shadowed areas of the dunes in *Desert Sand* on page 67.

SALT TEXTURES

Cover a large area with a wash, then sprinkle salt over it. When the wash has dried, brush the salt away. Tiny snowflake patterns will remain. Do the same thing with sand.

Knife Strokes on Wet Paper

In painting certain types of subjects on smooth paper—light tree trunks, for instance, or sunlit grass—a dull knife can be used as an effective tool while the paper is still damp or even wet. Different kinds of lines can be produced by holding the knife at different angles. Use a plowing or burnishing stroke rather than scraping or shoving.

If the knife is held almost vertically so that only the point touches the paper, it will make a thin line. When you lower it so it forms a more acute angle with the paper, a wider segment of the blade touches the paper and draws a wider line. If necessary, you can make a line as much as half an inch wide, but the section nearest the handle will probably be rather ragged.

If you want a dark line on one side of the white line, tip the knife to prevent its catching in the paper, and slant it so that the paint which was in its path will pile up on either right or left side.

If you want a dark line instead of a light one, make sure that the paper is really wet, not just damp. Hold the knife as you would hold a razor blade in shaving so that it will dig into the surface of the paper slightly. When the surface is roughened this way, it acts like blotting paper. The wet paint, attracted to the roughened mark on the paper, closes in behind the knife, thus producing a dark line.

I have sometime used a fingernail or a coin to make both light and dark lines in partly dried washes. However, a dull knife is better. The knife can produce a more delicate and more easily controlled line than a brush in these circumstances and will sometimes carry color from a wet spot over onto a dry one.

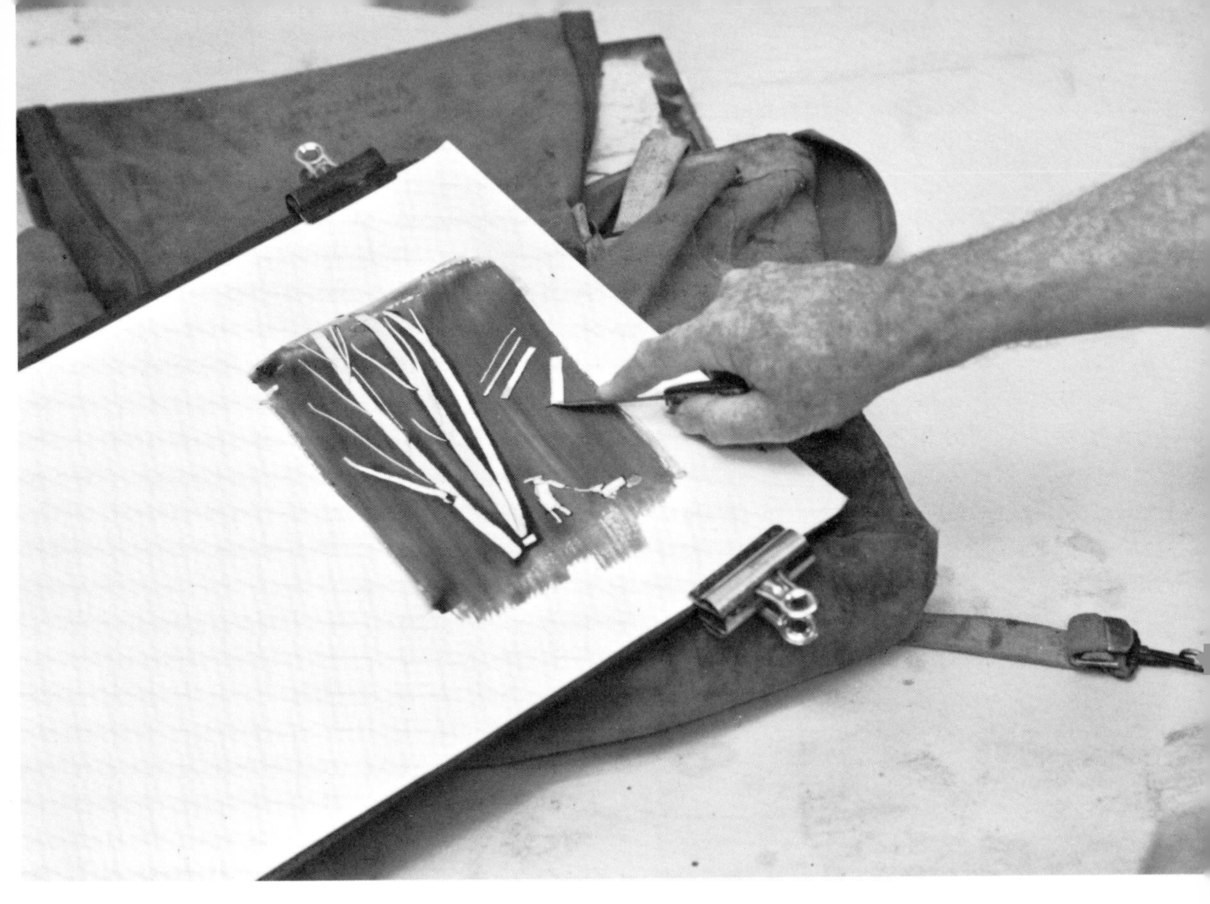

Light lines, dark lines, thin lines, and broad lines can be made with a knife in a wet wash. The photograph shows how the knife was held to make a broad light stroke.

This sketch was made in a few seconds on smooth paper. A dark wash was first brushed in place, then the lines were quickly scraped out with an ordinary penknife. Examples of knife strokes can also be seen in *Redwoods, Santa Cruz,* on page 98.

Calligraphy

The dictionary definition of calligraphy is "beautiful writing," but in watercolor technique calligraphic lines are symbols, or readily identifiable signs, for objects, qualities, textures, or anything else the artist wants to suggest without stating explicitly. They have been used with great skill by artists in many ages, from the ancient Egyptians, the Persians, and the Orientals, to modern painters like Matisse and Dufy. The most successful calligraphic symbols are not realistic drawings on a small scale but abstract lines, direction signs, or spots that label the subject, ignoring details that are obviously known by all.

When should you use calligraphy in a painting? Not in a picture that's a complete rendering of a realistic subject. That would merely be repeating yourself. If, however, you have vague areas of color scattered around the paper in patterns that may seem

The Joe Doaks House—CALLIGRAPHIC STYLE

In this approach to the Joe Doaks house I've used patches of selective color and tied them together with calligraphic lines that indicate clouds, pine trees, shingles, grass, and foliage.

CALLIGRAPHIC SYMBOLS

Chinese painters use calligraphic symbols, as do modern cartoonists. With a few lines it is possible to suggest much. The viewer fills in the missing information without difficulty.

L'Opéra BY RAOUL DUFY

COURTESY PHILLIPS MEMORIAL GALLERY, WASHINGTON, D. C.

Bright color patterns and calligraphic drawing are characteristics of Dufy's style.

abstract and unrelated to nature, the addition of a few calligraphic lines can establish miscellaneous areas as clouds, trees, water, rocks, buildings, or whatever you choose to make them. Besides giving a suggestion of realism to abstract color chords, calligraphic lines can sometimes pull together a picture that seems almost hopeless.

There can be as much or as little calligraphy in a picture as you choose. You may add just a few lines to one picture or you may do a whole picture in calligraphic style. Although calligraphy is sometimes overdone by contemporary painters, it can be very effective when used with skill and restraint.

Unpainted Intervals

One type of watercolor particularly suited to smooth paper is the picture in which spots of color are surrounded by large areas of white paper. Although the pictures may be realistic in subject, the effective arrangement of color areas and unpainted intervals is essentially a problem in abstract design. The pattern and order and size of the areas left unpainted are just as important as those which are painted. Such diverse painters as Paul Cézanne and John Singer Sargent used white paper very effectively in their watercolor sketches, and Paul Gill and Charles Demuth developed distinctive personal styles based on the skillful use of white paper. The technique is also very popular with contemporary illustrators.

Paul Gill, whose *Percé, Canada* is reproduced on page 79, filled most of the paper with color in a quite realistic way in his early watercolors. His experiments with white paper intervals began accidentally. In painting a scene directly from nature, he saw, between posts, a lake and sky that seemed almost white. He merely

Houses BY CHARLES DEMUTH

COURTESY CURRIER GALLERY OF ART, MANCHESTER, N. H.

Fisherman's Wharf, San Francisco BY ELIOT O'HARA

related the posts, distance, and earth to each other. The effectiveness of the result made him realize that white paper could be used to suggest even the darkest areas of a scene.

For your own first experiment with this type of picture, determine in advance that you will leave, say, 50 percent of the paper absolutely white and pure. Plan the picture on a separate sheet, deciding in advance how you will dispose your dark areas. Sometimes just a stroke or two of the right color placed on one side of a penciled outline will indicate a rock or boat, particularly if the area (most of which is still white paper) is silhouetted against something dark on the opposite side. A sky may be given an implication of complete grayness if it starts with a hard line and

Percé, Canada BY PAUL L. GILL

Gill used white paper to suggest even the darkest areas.

fades out into white paper. Japanese prints use this fading out effect cleverly. A deep blue band is sometimes placed across the top of a picture to remind the viewer that all of the sky might have been blue.

When your painting is completed, study it critically. Have you actually left at least 50 percent of the paper white within the picture? Or did you paint a small, tight, realistic watercolor, with all areas covered, floating in a sea of white paper? If you did that, the white paper is nothing more than a mat. You'd better try again.

If your finished picture has an anemic look, you may have used too many light colors and worked too long and too cautiously. This type of painting comes off best when it is done with vigor and confidence.

Opaque Watercolor and Related Mediums

SO FAR we have been discussing the basic techniques for painting transparent watercolors, or *aquarelles.* When a painter speaks of watercolors, he generally means aquarelles. The transparency of the medium is so highly prized that many watercolorists are scornful of anyone who uses opaque Chinese White for more than an occasional highlight. Nevertheless, opaque watercolor, or *gouache,* is a perfectly legitimate medium. It was used by Daumier and Toulouse-Lautrec among others, and it is favored by many contemporary illustrators and designers. It is especially useful for commercial work because it can be handled much like oil—with changes and corrections made by overpainting—but it dries much faster than oil.

Kinds of Opaque Watercolor Mediums

Any type of paint that is soluble in water is a mucilaginous, or watercolor, medium. The main differences between the various watercolor mediums is in the vehicle, or binder, or adhesive, that holds the particles of ground pigment or dye together. Regular artists watercolors are suspended in an emulsion of gum arabic, or some similar substance. Gouache colors, sometimes sold as Designers Colors, are usually made with the same kind of binder, but a filler is added to give them body and make them opaque. Cheaper lines of opaque watercolor, sold as Poster Colors,

Quadrille at the Moulin Rouge

BY HENRI DE TOULOUSE-LAUTREC

COURTESY NATIONAL GALLERY OF ART, WASHINGTON, D. C. (CHESTER DALE COLLECTION)

Gouache on cardboard.

Showcard Colors, School Tempera, etc., are often made with whiting and a glue size.

In addition to these traditional watercolor mediums, there are several related mediums which can be mixed with water and used in ways that resemble oil as well as aquarelle and gouache. The principal ones in use today are casein and polymer, also called polymer tempera. Casein colors are suspended in an emulsion with

Two Houses Under a Viaduct BY CHARLES BURCHFIELD

COURTESY REHN GALLERIES

Burchfield's watercolors are often done with opaque dark colors in a gouache technique.

a milk base. They are thinned with water, but a casein painting can be varnished like an oil or overpainted with oil glazes. Polymer paints are suspended in one of the new plastic resin emulsions. They can be thinned with water for transparent watercolor techniques, or with one of several types of polymer mediums for gouache or oil techniques. Polymer paints and mediums can also be used in many other ways and are especially suitable for collage.

Most of the major manufacturers of artists colors produce lines of opaque watercolors and several offer lines of casein and polymer artists colors. Remember though that the cheaper colors for short-lived posters or for children's busy work are not meant for serious painting. Commercial polymer house paints were used by some artists before the artists polymer colors came on the market. The house paints may not be quite as brilliant, but are probably just as permanent as the artists colors—and much less expensive.

Materials and Equipment

SUPPORTS

The opaque mediums require a more solid painting base and a smoother, less absorbent surface than transparent watercolor. If you use paper, mount it first on a stiff cardboard—or buy it already mounted. Stretched canvas isn't particularly suitable for these mediums, but the commercially prepared canvas boards are. You can also use masonite, plaster wall board, or wood panels. Unless you buy already prepared supports, you should coat the surface with gesso before beginning to paint. You can mix your own gesso from whiting and glue, or you can buy it already mixed. The new polymer gesso, available in most art supply stores, is a good ground for any of these painting mediums.

Tinted papers have been traditionally popular for gouache. The light opaque colors can be very effective against dark papers with the color of the paper used as part of the composition, just as white paper is in aquarelle. Tinted papers are available in a wide range of colors, or you can make your own by using a ground coat of any color you choose. In fact, you can tone any painting surface by mixing polymer colors into the priming coat of polymer gesso.

BRUSHES AND PALETTE KNIVES

Most painters prefer oil brushes and palette knives for casein, gouache, and polymer painting because the colors are usually applied more heavily than in transparent watercolor and are manipulated much as oil colors are. However, if you are using polymer paints in aquarelle technique, you may prefer the softer watercolor brushes. Since the opaque colors dry and harden in the brush much faster than ordinary watercolors, it's a good idea to keep your brushes wet while in use and to wash them thoroughly when you have finished for the day. A special polymer paint remover is available for softening or removing hardened polymer paints, but once casein has hardened it is almost impossible to remove. Since casein is particularly hard on brushes, some painters keep a set of old, rather worn brushes for casein work.

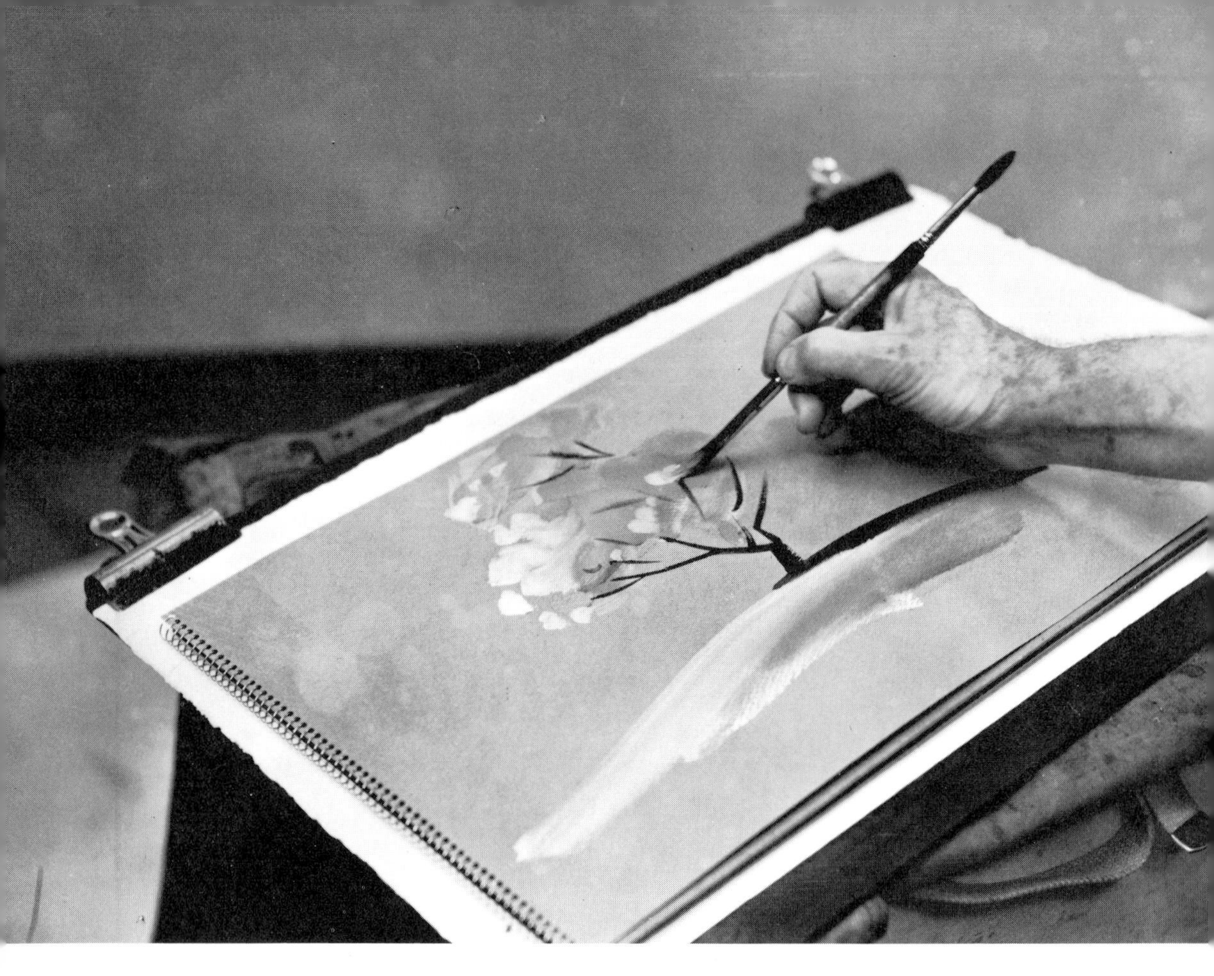

Gouache lends itself to interesting effects on tinted paper, particularly when the color of the paper is used as part of the design—as white paper is used in transparent watercolor.

PALETTE

A white butcher's tray—or some similar surface—makes a good palette for opaque watercolors. As for colors, you will want an assortment similar to those suggested for aquarelle. However, the finely ground colors that are particularly desirable for transparent washes are of no importance when colors are applied heavily or in layers. You can therefore add coarsely ground colors like Viridian, Cerulean Blue, Raw Sienna, Manganese Blue, and Davy's Gray to your opaque palette.

The palette arrangement can follow whatever pattern you worked out for your regular watercolors. One note of warning: Since gouache, casein, and polymer paints dry out so much faster than transparent watercolors, it might be wise to be a bit stingier with the amounts you place on your palette until you learn to gauge how much you are likely to need for a particular painting session.

MEDIUMS AND VARNISHES

Several varnishes and special mediums are available for use with casein and polymer paints. The mediums are used either in place of or together with water to thin the colors as they are mixed and applied. Some mediums impart a glossy texture to the paint surface when dry, others leave a matte surface. Varying degrees of glossiness can be obtained by experimenting with mixtures. Varnishes are applied over the painting surface, sometimes as a form of protection, sometimes to adjust the surface gloss. Some mediums can be used as varnishes, some cannot. Better check the manufacturer's directions, especially with the new polymer products.

Opaque Techniques

Assuming you have already tried the exercises suggested for learning basic watercolor techniques, you can follow much the same routine in trying out any or all of the opaque watercolor mediums. You will soon discover for yourself that there are things you can do with aquarelle that you can't do with gouache or casein, but then gouache, casein, and polymer will produce textures and colors you will never get with aquarelle. All you can do is experiment until your own experience tells you which mediums and techniques suit you best.

GOUACHE

You don't have to invest in special gouache colors to begin your experiments with gouache technique. Just mix enough Chinese White with your regular watercolors to make them opaque. Try a variety of brushstrokes and textures first. Apply the colors in thin washes, in medium washes, and as thickly as possible. Use a palette knife to apply and manipulate the thick paint. When areas have dried, paint light colors over dark ones, dark over light, thick over thin, and vice versa.

Once you have got the feel of the medium, repaint the Joe Doaks house again—or some other picture—in gouache. One thing you will soon discover is that colors don't dry the way you expect them to. Even if you have adjusted to the idea that in watercolor painting colors always dry lighter than they appear when wet, you will still be surprised at the way an underpainted color can affect a surface color. You may or may not like the chalkiness of gouache colors. Some do, some don't. If you don't, try using less white and more pale yellow (or Naples Yellow, which is a mixture of Yellow Ochre and white).

CASEIN

Casein can be used in many different ways. It can be thinned with water until it approaches transparency or it can be applied in a thick impasto. It can be left with a matte finish like a gouache or varnished like an oil. The painting can be done in a simple direct way or it can be built up with transparent glazes of casein or oil or polymer over a casein underpainting. It can also be combined in various other mixed media techniques.

For your first experiments with casein, however, treat it as opaque watercolor and follow the routine suggested for gouache. Once you have got used to the idiosyncrasies of casein as gouache, you can go on and experiment with impastos, glazes, varnishes, and other specialized techniques, including some you may want to make up yourself.

One thing you're bound to discover about casein is that it dries very quickly, much faster than oil, and with more determination than watercolor. This is sometimes an advantage—on painting trips where you have to pack up and move on in a short time, for instance. However, it also means you have to work fast, even when you're using an oil technique.

POLYMER

Polymer, or polymer tempera, is the newest—and possibly the most flexible—of all painting mediums now available. A number of painters have been experimenting with a variety of formulas for years, mixing dry pigments and dyes with mediums and emulsions made for other commercial purposes, or using the acrylic house paints that have been on the market for some time. By the mid-1960's, however, several brands of artists polymer colors were available—

Tidal #6

BY JAMES TWITTY

COURTESY THE CORCORAN GALLERY OF ART, WASHINGTON, D. C.

Acrylic and sand.

under a variety of coined trade names—in art supply stores throughout the country.

Polymer colors are products of modern chemistry and their formulation is beyond the comprehension of most non-chemists. They are said to be exceptionally stable and permanent—and there's no reason to doubt it. However, not all of the brands available are based on the same chemical formulas. There are, therefore, certain differences in the properties and characteristics of specific brands. Several manufacturers have trial sets of small jars or tubes of color and medium, with booklets that describe their polymer products and tell how to use them. It might be worthwhile to experiment with one or more of these trial sets to get the feel of the new medium and to check the characteristics of several brands yourself. Be sure to read the descriptive booklets carefully for clues to differences and similarities.

In experimenting with polymer you can again follow the routine suggested for gouache. In the case of polymer colors, however, they can be thinned with water and used to achieve the same kinds of effects you get with aquarelle—transparent washes, wet-in-wet, drybrush, and the like. With less dilution, the colors will have the opaque appearance of gouache. They can be applied thickly like oils, or can be mixed with various types of mediums for matte, satin, gloss, or rich impasto surfaces. The finish can be protected, adjusted, or isolated with a matte or gloss varnish.

Pelican Watch BY ELIOT O'HARA

Collage was used for this painting. Rice paper was attached to masonite with polymer transparent medium, then overpainted with watercolor.

Polymer paints and mediums are also suitable for use with other materials in creating collages (discussed separately) and in many other ways. Sand, for instance, was mixed with acrylic—which is much the same as the paints now called polymer—to achieve interesting surface textures in James Twitty's *Tidal #6,* on page 87.

COLLAGE

Collage—sometimes called assemblage or montage—is the name for pictures put together by pasting papers, cloths, or any other materials to a surface which may be painted or not according to the design or whim of the artist. The word also is used to refer to the method of doing this. In the sense that most of the adhesives used for collage are soluble in water, you could call it a watercolor medium. It also combines well with any of the water-soluble mediums. The success of a collage depends on how well the materials chosen are arranged and put together in terms of shape, color, and textures.

Almost any type of material can be cut into shapes and mounted on a masonite board, a laminated wood panel, or some other sturdy painting surface. However, if you want your collages to last, avoid using newspapers that turn yellow, inks that fade, or other elements you know to be impermanent. Be sure, too, that your adhesive is permanent. Flour paste and rubber cement have their uses, but not for this kind of work. Wax, oil, glue, gums of various kinds, egg yolk, lacquer, and casein are among the mediums that have been used as adhesives for mounting and painting collages, but the new polymer mediums seem to be best. They are transparent, elastic, and permanent.

Aside from worrying about the permanence of materials, there are no rules for collage. Just try anything that occurs to you. If you don't like it, change it. Paint over it; cover it with a translucent paper to veil it; or obliterate it completely by using a more interesting opaque texture over it.

The painting *Pelican Watch*, on page 88, is a collage built up with many pieces of rice paper stuck on a masonite panel using transparent polymer medium as adhesive. The masonite had first been coated with white dry pigment in polymer medium. After the base coat dried—in a half hour—the surface was again covered with polymer medium—transparent this time—and the work proceeded. Rice paper offers interesting textures for collage and is easy to use, but it is sometimes colored with fugitive dyes. For that reason, it is usually a good idea to paint over rice paper with permanent colors.

Techniques Relating to Special Subjects

IN PAINTING any subject derived from nature—whether you are painting on the spot or working from notes, sketches, photographs, and memory in your studio—you should begin by observing the scene and analyzing all the components that interest you. Sift them through your mind until you decide what you want to say about the scene, then plan your composition and paint the picture. With minor variations, that should hold true for any picture. Each artist must make his own decisions and find his own solutions to pictorial problems every time he paints a picture.

The suggestions in this chapter on how to deal with certain elements that turn up in many watercolors—trees, for instance—won't automatically solve any problems for you, but they may help you to find shortcuts.

Trees

Trees are a part of most landscapes. You will find them along city streets as well as country roads, and even a desert scene is likely to be punctuated by a giant cactus or two. So if you paint landscapes, you have to paint trees.

Some painters are able to suggest the general shape and idea of a tree when the composition just calls for a mass of unidentified greenery, but they get bogged down when they have to paint a particular tree or a group of trees of different kinds. Often all that is necessary is a shorthand symbol representing a tree—perhaps

Picacho and Cottonwoods BY ELIOT O'HARA

COLLECTION OF DR. WILLIAM E. MURPHY, WORCESTER, MASS.

a cone for a spruce tree or a column for a poplar—but sometimes a more detailed description is wanted. Either way, the more you know about the peculiarities of many different types of trees, the easier it will be to interpret the basic facts about a particular tree in a personal way that will interest the viewer.

If you are not already familiar with a wide variety of trees, from personal observation and from sketching them, now is the time to start studying them carefully. The illustrations on the next few pages suggest several ways of looking at trees as well as hints on how to paint them, but nothing will help as much as your own firsthand experience. Try to paint the same tree at different seasons and in different kinds of light, noting the overall silhouette, the way the branches relate to the trunks, the size and color of individual leaves, the color and density of the foliage in spring, summer, and fall, and the clearly outlined structure of the bare tree in winter. Note, too, the apparent differences of the colors, values, and textures of the leaves and bark, branches and trunk as the light changes. Foliage that is pale green or silver one moment may be dark green the next. The texture of the bark may be emphasized by light and shadow or reduced to a flat tone.

In your studies of trees, paint them as realistically as you can at first, but once you know what the tree looks like, try to suggest all you know about it as sparingly as possible.

STRUCTURE

Before painting a tree, try to visualize its underlying structure. There are many ways to do this. You may think of it as a skeleton, for instance, or as an abstract design. This sketch visualizes five types of trees in terms of pipelines supplying water to communities, which is not too farfetched since the flow of life-giving sap within the tree is fed by water absorbed by the roots and is carried to each of the branches, twigs, and leaves.

Diagram A, which suggests a row of houses along Main Street, corresponds to a pine tree. Diagram B, with its cluster of houses far from the water supply, is like a palm tree. The large tanks supplying small individual houses in Diagram C suggest the giant saguaro cactus. Apple trees and willows are much like Diagram D, which resembles a cluster of houses close to one source of supply. Diagram E, which resembles a beech or poplar, shows several houses on separate pipelines far from the trunk line.

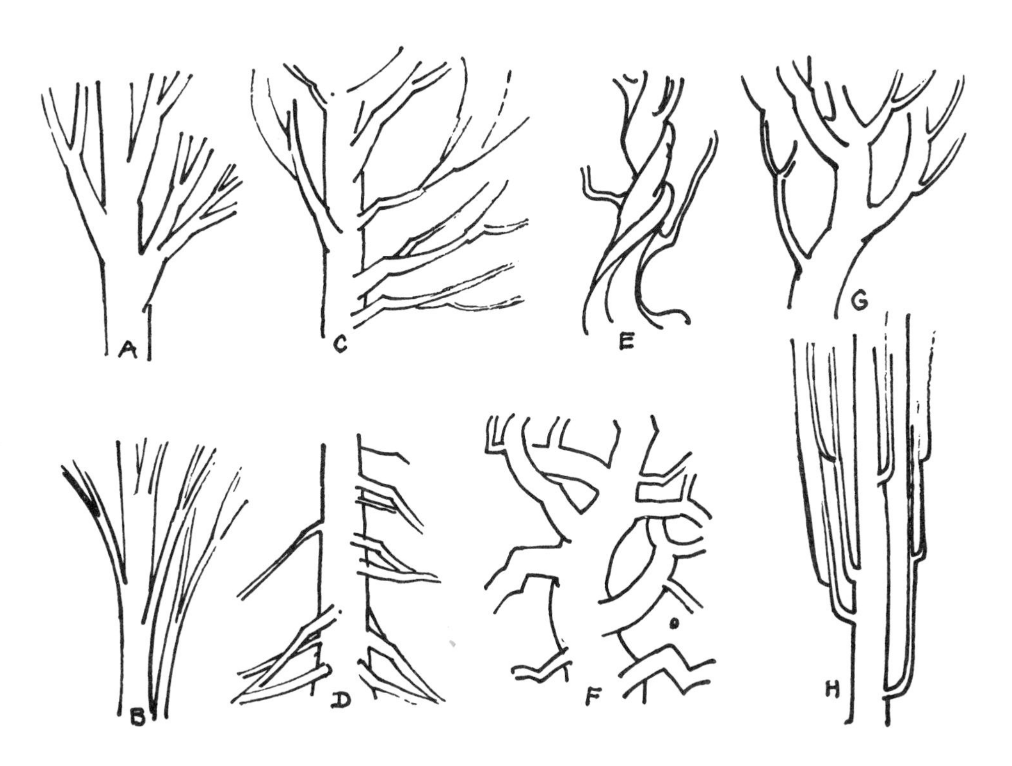

BRANCH ARTICULATION

To understand the anatomy of any tree, you must know how its branches are attached to the main trunk and to each other. These diagrams show some common forms of branch articulation.

A. Straight limbs and Y-shaped joints are generally characteristic of elm trees.

B. Other trees, the ash for example, also have Y-shaped joints, but the limbs tend to curve outward from the trunk.

C. The forked joints of the maple are more U-shaped than Y-shaped and the limbs curve gently upward.

D. The branches of some kinds of pine trees form right angles with the trunk, then curve upward or downward.

E. The joints of trees like the cedar and the myrtle seem to twist out of a spiral or corkscrew formation.

F. The branches of apple trees and oak trees jut out at right angles from the trunk, then curve upward or downward.

G. The white pine has Y-shaped junctures with inward curving branches.

H. Poplar branches are almost vertical and parallel with the trunk, to which they are attached at right angles.

Another approach to learning to see and to paint trees. Each tree is represented in the top row by a few squiggles or a symbolic shape that suggests the tree. The lines in the middle row are brushstrokes utilized in the paintings of the trees in the bottom row.

CYPRESS

The foliage was painted with a flat brush, the branches and twigs with a round pointed small brush.

LOMBARDY POPLAR

Quick, dry, vertical strokes were brushed toward the top. The branches were indicated with a thin round brush, or rigger.

MAPLE

A big brush described the foliage with elliptical fuzzy strokes. Notice the spherical solid shape of the foliage and the dark holes in it.

WILLOW

A dry brush dragged lightly downward makes the willow weep and drip.

FIR

Arrowheads painted with dark tube color and almost no water indicate the branches and needles of the fir tree.

OAK

The branches come in strange combinations of angles and arcs; the bark has warts; and the foliage is best indicated by patting.

BIRCH

The trunks are white or very light where the bark is peeled off, and there are dark triangles where the branches are attached to the trunk.

CEDAR

A dry brush full of dark color pushed upward splays out to describe the silhouette of the cedar.

ELM

In summer, when full of sap, elm branches droop more than in winter. Notice the lozenge-shaped air holes between the branches.

APPLE

The trunk of an apple tree usually leans one way or the other, and there is nearly always a stub or two where a branch was sawed off.

PALM

The fronds are made with a dry brush and the same kind of stroke used for a fir tree.

A VARIETY OF TREES

Notice the extent to which the trees on these pages differ in silhouette, structure, branch articulation, and massing of foliage. Note, too, that a variety of technical means have been used to indicate the play of light and shadow, the color and density of the foliage, and the texture of trunk and branches. All of the rough

brushing techniques are useful in painting trees. Most of the trees shown here were painted with a wet brush and the dry brush effects were achieved by varying the speed of brushing or the direction of the stroke. However, the bare tree in the group above was painted with a brush so dry that the hairs separated into four or five clusters. The center tree in the same group was painted with a wet brush and then blotted with a clean dry brush.

Redwoods, Santa Cruz BY ELIOT O'HARA

Painting a Forest

In painting the interior of a forest focus on the confusion of detail rather than on one or two particular trees.

In *Redwoods, Santa Cruz,* I was not painting portraits of individual trees, but effects of light and shade and vaporous mists among the tall dark giants of the West Coast. The sun-streaked opening in the woods provides the viewer with an entrance into the picture and a sense of seeing the trees from a slight distance while in the very midst of them. The nearest trees are dark and details of texture and structure are indicated, but not so specifically that the eye will concentrate on them. The trees to the side are dark blurs against lighter blurs, suggesting undefined details hidden by smoky mists. Although the trees in the distance are barely indicated, they imply an extensive stand of trees stretching into the distance.

In painting this picture some of the white areas of sky were preserved by brushing around them, but some areas of mist were sponged out while the wash was still damp. Many of the small white strokes among the dark trees were scraped out with a knife.

alm Patterns BY ELIOT O'HARA

Sea Gulls BY ELIOT O'HARA

Birds in Flight

In paintings where birds are seen only as specks against the sky, it is usually enough to devise a calligraphic symbol that suggests the direction of flight. Close-ups of birds in flight are something else again. It is necessary, of course, to study the characteristics of whatever bird or birds you are painting, but the degree of accuracy of detail will depend on whether you want to do ornithological studies or quick impressions of color in motion.

Whatever your intention, you should understand how a bird flies. Contrary to what many people believe, the wings do not paddle like the fins of fish, which push the water back and the fish ahead, working much like the oars of a rowboat. In flying, birds generally use a flapping motion, stroking up and back, down and forward. As the wings stroke down and forward, air is pushed under and

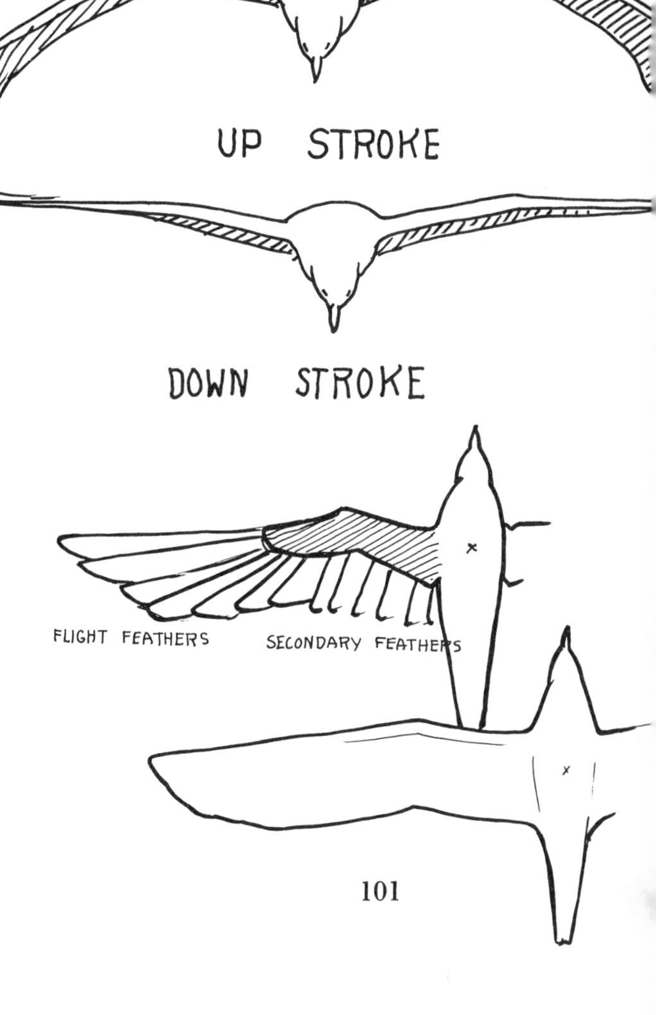

In flight the joint of the wing is bent on the upstroke and the flexible points of the feathers are turned downward. On the downstroke, the wing is flatter and the tips of the feathers bend upward.

The wings are attached to the body near the center of gravity (x). Gulls have long narrow wings with large flight feathers along the outer edge of the wing and smaller secondary feathers close to the body. Although the shape and proportions vary in other types of birds, the principles remain the same.

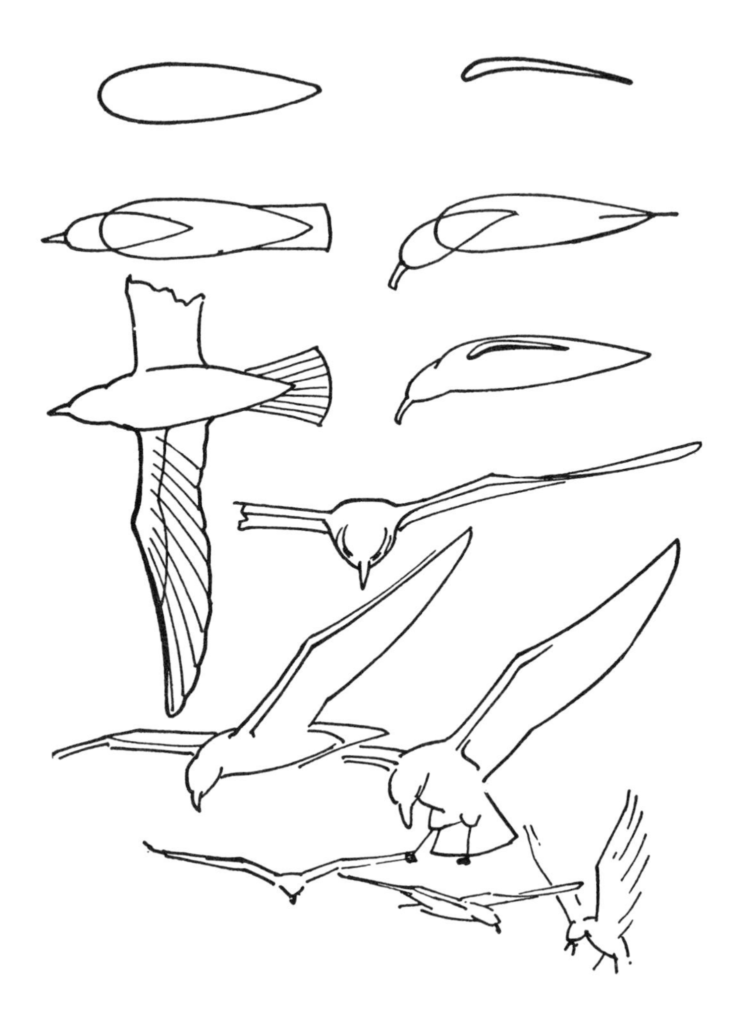

FLIGHT ENGINEERING OF BIRDS

The basic shape of a bird's body in flight is like a horizontal teardrop, slightly flattened on the bottom (top left). The sliver shape, top right, is a cross section of a bird's wing, convex on top, concave underneath.

The next few diagrams show side views of body, head, and tail, with the tail in different positions. The rest of the sketches show the structure of a gull's wing and the way it relates to the body of the gull in flight—as seen from several angles. When a bird comes in for a landing, it lowers its flaps and landing gear. The legs drop, the wings backstroke, and the feet open as the bird hits the ground.

ahead of the bird and it rides on this volume of compressed air. The tail and the flight feathers (the large feathers on the outer part of the trailing edge of the wings) are used much like the rudder and flaps of an airplane to control speed and direction. The smaller, close-fitting feathers that cover the leading edge of the wings help to give them the smoothly rounded airfoil shape that moves through the air with the greatest of ease. In flight, with feet tucked up underneath like the retractable landing gear they are, the curve of the head and body resembles a horizontal teardrop. In addition to being a good design for flight because it offers a minimum of resistance to air, the shape suggests forward motion, even standing still. That is why it has been adopted for all sorts of streamlined designs from airplanes and automobiles to kitchen appliances.

All birds that fly, chickens included, have the same parts (head, body, tail, wings, feet, beak, feathers), but the shapes and proportions of the various parts vary greatly. The wings may be short and broad, long and broad, or long and narrow, with distinctive arrangements of flight feathers depending on the bird's usual habitat and activities. The short wings of the chicken won't take it far from the ground no matter how hard it flaps them, but the long, broad wings of the eagle are designed for soaring at great altitudes

Gulls in Flight BY ELIOT O'HARA

Gulls Feeding BY HENRY GEORGE KELLER

COURTESY THE CLEVELAND MUSEUM OF ART, J. H. WADE COLLECTION

with only the slightest movement of the wings, and the long narrow wings of the gull are perfectly adapted for soaring, gliding, and diving.

Gulls are fun to watch and their activities offer lots of good material for paintings. In flight they create graceful patterns against the sea and the sky as they soar and glide, swoop and dive, land unhurriedly on the water, swim for a while, then take off again. On shore they may be less graceful, but they are amusing as they clap their wings excitedly at the sight of food and walk leisurely away when well fed. As a gull observer you may see other things worth noting—their contemplation of intruders, for instance—but in any one painting you should restrict yourself to one point of view.

In painting gulls in flight, try to organize a pattern of their flight. They may hover first, then swoop, usually in a spiral. Create the basic pattern, then build the gulls along this trajectory. The gulls may appear white in sunlight, but on the dark side of the feathers blue shadows will probably be reflected from the sky, the clouds, or the water. If the shadows are influenced by rocks or sand, however, they will be warmer. To emphasize the whiteness of the birds, paint the rocks or the ocean darker than they seem.

Gull Forms BY ELIOT O'HARA

Collage of polymer medium and watercolor.

Sea and Surf

The sea has attracted and challenged man for thousands of years. It has been a source of food and recreation, a means of livelihood, and a highway to adventure, international commerce, and imperial conquest. No wonder it has been painted so often.

Trying to paint the restless, ever-moving sea is also a challenge. Every summer thousands of painters flock to coastal areas to interpret the sea and surf, and each artist has his own way of looking at it. Some rhapsodize, some malign it, some merely reproduce it—or try to.

The sea washes a wide variety of shorelines, each with its own distinctive characteristics. Wave-cut cliffs and strange rock formations line one shore; marshy tidelands another. A beach may be a graceful arc within a sheltered cove or an endless stretch of sand dunes along the ocean. The sand can be almost white, or it may be pink, or orange, or brown, or even black, as it is in some places in the Caribbean. There may be no sand at all, only rocks and boulders, or smooth little pebbles like those you find on the Riviera. The water may appear blue, or green, or gray, or some other color. In fact, it will usually appear to be different colors in different areas, depending on its relative opacity or transparency, the reflected sky color, and whether the sea is rough or calm.

Sunken Ledges BY CHARLES H. WOODBURY

COURTESY MUSEUM OF FINE ARTS, BOSTON

Woodbury's painting, a watercolor on smooth paper, skillfully conveys both the deep pull below the waves and the frothiness of their crests.

The Great Wave BY HOKUSAI

COURTESY MUSEUM OF FINE ARTS, BOSTON

Woodblock print.

To me, the very essence of surf is continual movement, restless and varied. In a painting this can only be implied, and it isn't an easy thing to do. I have seen pictures by very popular seascape painters in which the waves do not move. Like still photographers, the artist has caught a moment of arrested movement. This is true even of the great Japanese artist Hokusai's dramatic woodblock print of a wave. Its fingers will menace the boat beneath until the end of time—but the wave will never fall.

Before trying to paint the movement of waves, we have to understand something of how they behave. Waves move through the water in alternate crests and troughs, but the particles of water remain in more or less the same place, moving up and down, as you know if you have ever been swimming in the surf. What happens is something like what happens when a garden hose is flipped. The hump moves, but the hose itself remains in about the same place.

At sea the waves are equally steep front and back, but as they approach a beach, the sand beneath causes friction that retards the movement of the underwater part of the wave. The top, moving faster, overtakes the lower part and eventually falls, making the wave "break." As a breaker crests, the line is concave at the rear and convex in front.

Where the shore is a curve of beach with a wall of rocks at each end, the friction caused by the water moving against the rocks will slow down the movement of the waves at either end, but in the center they will travel faster, forming an arc that roughly parallels the curve of the shore. Many painters, seeing the semicircular banks of foam, paint them as they see them, letting their brushstrokes follow the crests of the waves. If we want to suggest the movement of waves, this is a mistake. The eye will follow the direction of the brushstrokes, leading the path of vision around the cove rather than following the movement of the waves toward the shore. The brushstrokes should move with the waves, not across them. The strokes can themselves be symbols of movement, like the comet or polliwog-shaped strokes in the illustration of wave movements. This shape suggests both the appearance of the surf and the direction it is moving. Another way to suggest movement is to indicate a progression, one wave starting to break, then another a little more advanced. You don't need too many. One or two may be enough.

Remember, too, that waves are seen in perspective. If their apparent movement is toward the shore, they will seem larger nearby. If the wind is from the side and the waves appear to move sideways, they will have a vanishing point. When the high sky is dark and the low sky light, the near sides of the waves will be darker than the tops.

So far we have been discussing surf in relation to sandy beaches, but when a wave hits a rock or a cliff, all sorts of strange things happen. The waves may ride up over one rock and break just beyond it, explode against another, and barely dribble over others. It depends on the slant of the rock and the angle at which the wave hits it. Often the surf along a rocky shore will be affected by submerged ledges and rocks as well as by the visible formations.

There are many possible approaches to painting the sea and the surf. If the sea interests you, the best thing you can do is to study

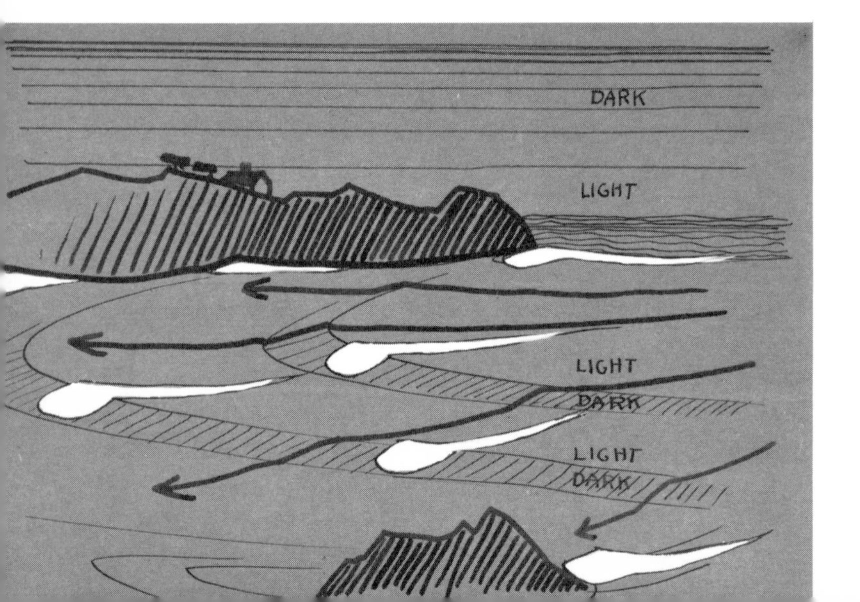

The white shapes like polliwogs or comets are less obvious directional signals than arrows and more suitable symbols for surf. They help to keep the brushstrokes moving in the direction the waves take and discourage any tendency to emphasize the crests of the waves.

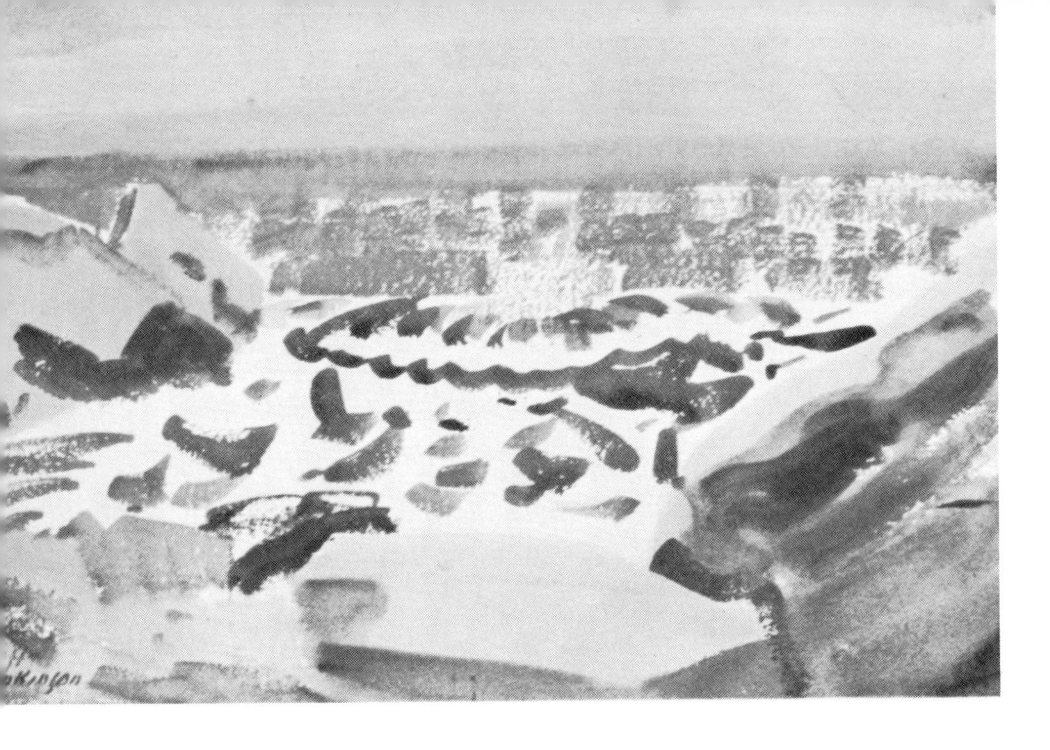

Surf and Sun BY CHARLES HOPKINSON

Hopkinson uses color and calligraphy in a quick, sketchy style that suggests bright sunlight on an ever-changing pattern of foaming surf.

it at first hand. Make dozens—or hundreds—of quick sketches to try to catch its ever-changing movements and moods. Then try to recapture what you have learned about the sea and surf in more carefully thought-out studio pictures, in different styles and mannerisms. In the long run you may decide the "quickies" come closer to the truth about the surf than anything you try in the studio.

Sea and Surf BY ELIOT O'HARA

Reflections in Water and on Wet Pavement

In general, there are three kinds of wet reflections for a painter to worry about: reflections in smooth water, reflections in rippled water, and reflections on wet surfaces such as pavements. Actually, there are infinite variations on each. There's the color of the water. Is it blue, green, gray, black, brown, yellow, red, or iridescent? Is it clear? Can you see the bottom? Is the bottom sandy, pebbled, rocky, covered with coral? Are there shadows on it? Or is the water opaque and muddy, perhaps covered with an oil slick? Is the sun adding sparkling highlights to the surface or has an overcast sky made everything seem flat and dull? Each variant adds new problems for you to worry about along with the reflections. There are, however, a few things that will usually hold true.

Reflections in smooth water are much like reflections in a mirror. The objects reflected are seen in reverse. Under ideal conditions the reflection may be a perfect mirror image, but usually there is some distortion due to the movement of the water and other factors. A good way to study reflections in smooth water is to set up a toy village on a table, using a mirror or piece of glass as the neighborhood pond or cove. With such a setup you can study the reflections from many different eye levels. You will discover that

Reflections, Gloucester BY ELIOT O'HARA

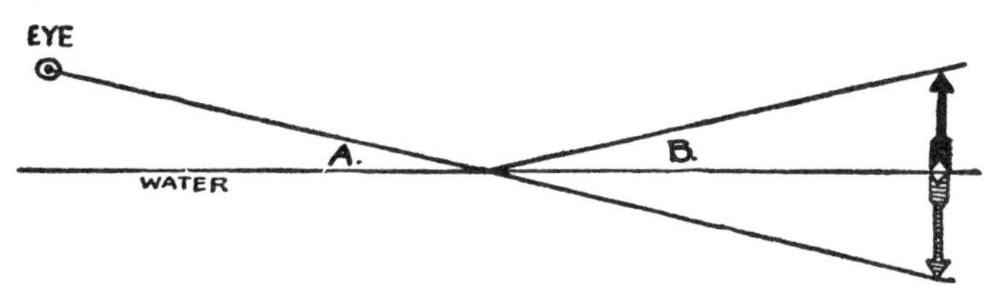

ANGLE OF INCIDENCE A. EQUALS ANGLE OF REFLECTION B.

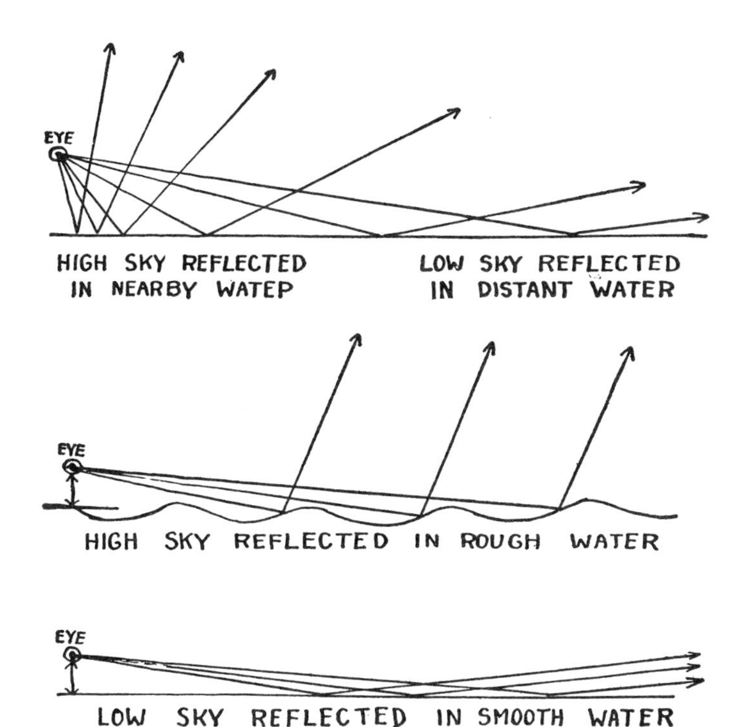

ANGLES OF INCIDENCE AND REFLECTION

These diagrams may help you to visualize some of the factors that control reflections. The angle of incidence is determined by the eye level of the viewer who sees the water; in other words, the eye level of the painter. That angle determines the angle of reflection and the baseline on which all things reflected are reversed. Sky reflections are also determined by the angles of incidence and reflection.

the angle from which you view the water (or mirror) affects what you see reflected. If you look down into the mirror—as if you were standing on a cliff looking into the water below—you will see your own reflection and probably little else. If you step back or bend down so that your eye focuses on the water at a more acute angle, your own reflection disappears and you see reflections of objects along the far side of the shore. Exactly what you see depends on the angle at which your eye meets the water.

The reflections of boats or other objects actually on the water will be seen as reverse extensions of the objects themselves, but trees, houses, rocks, hills, and the like will not be reflected from the shoreline unless their base is right on the water's edge. Things situated beyond the shoreline will be reversed on a baseline equivalent to the level of the water if it extended inland to a point directly beneath them. At some eye levels, therefore, you will see certain objects clearly, but they will not be reflected; from other angles, you will see the reflections of objects that are hidden from sight.

Reflections in rough water are like reflections in a mirror, too—a broken mirror, or perhaps a number of mirrors tilted in different directions. If you take a small hand mirror and tilt it at various angles, you will see what happens with reflections in waves and ripples. The top of the wave will reflect the low sky or the trunk of a tree; the near side will reflect the high sky or the top of the tree. Since we can't see the far side of the wave, it reflects nothing.

Wet pavements and similar surfaces often have depressions in which pools of water form. Reflections in such pools follow the same pattern as in any body of smooth water. Where the surface is only damp, the reflections will be diffused, as the simplified sketch shows. If the surface is uneven, the reflections may also be distorted.

A. CLEAR REFLECTIONS IN POOLS
B. DIFFUSED IMAGES IN WET PAVEMENT

Skies

The sky is an important element in most landscape paintings. It may be clear or cloudy, as bright as a picture postcard, or as dark as a winter's night. It can be any color at all. As we've all observed, the light of the sky at different times of day and under various atmospheric conditions may appear red, orange, yellow, or green, as well as gray, blue, and violet. At sunrise or sunset the changing colors in the sky often range through the whole spectrum in a matter of minutes.

Obviously, there are no rules for painting skies. If you're working directly from nature and want to paint skies as you see them, you have to work fast. It's a rare day when the sky remains the same for the length of time it takes a wash to dry. If it's a day with scudding clouds or with thunderheads building, the cloud patterns will change between the moment you look at them and the moment you touch your brush to the paper. The only way to deal with this problem is to practice making quick sketches that try to do no more than catch a mood or a fleeting impression of a transient moment. This works well for other constantly changing subjects—such as surf, or moving traffic, or large crowds—as well as for skies.

Annapolis Winter BY ELIOT O'HARA

Snow on the Mesa BY ELIOT O'HARA

COURTESY FINE ARTS GALLERY, SAN DIEGO

If you're painting skies from memory—not as you see them, but as you want them to be in your picture—the problem is different. You can plan the kind of sky that will contribute most to the design and mood of the picture. You may want a very simple background such as the gray sky in *Along the Seine,* on page 152, where the sky is used as a backdrop, a flat plane behind the foreground planes. Or you may want to make the sky the main focus of the composition as in *Snow on the Mesa.* The sky can add important color notes that key the color scheme of the picture, and it can dramatize whatever mood you want to express.

Wet blending is often used in painting skies because it so easily suggests the soft transitions of sky tones and cloud forms, but don't feel that every sky has to be an exercise in wet blending. Try any approach that suits you for a particular subject.

Crowds of People

Any crowd of people is a mass of individuals, each with his own personality, his own problems, and his own destination—or lack of one. But when you look at a crowd, you don't see the individuals in it, you see the crowd itself—bustling, ambling, or waiting; standing or sitting; relaxed, happy, jubilant, excited, tense, angry, expectant, or indifferent. The individuals are anonymous, but they are part of a time, a place, and a mood.

In painting a crowd, whether it is the subject of the picture or only a secondary element in the composition, concentrate on whatever it is that distinguishes this crowd from other crowds. If it's a rush-hour mob hurrying to or from work along a busy thoroughfare, the essence of the crowd is movement. Diagonal brushstrokes will indicate the foreward lean of people in a hurry and sharp contrasts of color and value will emphasize the feeling of activity. A stadium full of cheering football fans may look like hundreds of tiny blobs of color. To keep the stadium jumping, again use strong contrasts of light and dark values, warm and cool colors, or juxtapose vivid complementaries of equal value. A crowded beach may be just a jumble of suntanned bodies, some partially silhouetted against sky and surf. A theatre audience can be a vague blur of heads and faces, such as Raoul Dufy describes in *L'Opéra,* on page 76. A few looping calligraphic lines say all that is necessary about the elegant dress circle.

In city landscapes, groups of people are often a secondary but important part of the scene. The figures in *Eros in Piccadilly* are of

Winter Day in Calcutta BY ELIOT O'HARA

COURTESY OF MR. AND MRS. CARL SIGNEL

no particular interest in themselves, but without them the busy London street would seem ominously empty. On the other hand, the dark-skinned, white-robed figures of *Winter Day in Calcutta,* like the cows wandering among them, do attract our attention because, for most of us at least, they are not a familiar sight. Still the picture does not focus on the individuals, but on the characteristics of the crowd in this particular place.

Whatever kind of crowd you are painting, don't make the mistake of trying to do a group portrait—that will only distract the viewer. You can easily indicate crowds of people with a few torso-sized brushstrokes, a couple of well-placed blobs for heads, and here and there a suggestion of legs, feet, arms, or other details. You don't have to supply a full set of parts for each figure. If you imply the nature of the crowd, the viewer will fill in the missing details.

Figures in a Landscape BY ELIOT O'HARA

This picture demonstrates one way to handle large groups of figures in a landscape. In this case I brushed in vague areas suggesting the average color of clothing worn on a rainy day in this city, somewhere in the Middle East. I used a large varnishing brush and worked with great speed to prevent the careful, too precise craftsmanship that could turn brushstrokes into individuals. Although I counted at least 32 figure-sized strokes, I allowed only nine heads for the whole crowd. Then, using casual, calligraphic outlines, I tied together unrelated patches of color and indicated a few details—the flowing robes, a woman and baby, a couple of umbrellas—to characterize this particular crowd.

Eros in Piccadilly BY ELIOT O'HARA

COURTESY AMERICAN ARTIST MAGAZINE

Portrait of José de Creeft BY ELIOT O'HARA

Portraits

Few watercolor painters seem inclined to paint portraits in this medium, perhaps because it seems harder to correct the traditional "something" that sitter and friends are always finding wrong with the mouth. Nevertheless, the quick watercolor sketch is an excellent medium for catching the fleeting characteristic expressions that glimmer briefly and die during long hours of posing for an oil portrait. When a watercolor portrait really "comes off," it has a directness rarely seen in oils.

Portraits differ from other types of painting in one important respect: The picture should look like the subject. You may rearrange a landscape to suit your idea of a good design and hardly anyone will care, but if you rearrange your sitter's features, you may be sure that he (or she) will care. The picture may turn out to be an interesting psychological study of an unknown character, but if it's not recognizable as the sitter, it's not his portrait. How to get a likeness is another matter. Some painters do it easily, others

Portrait of a Young Woman

BY ELIOT O'HARA

Portrait of
Mrs. Theodore Eliot

BY WILLIAM H. CALFEE

Gouache on tinted paper.

get all the features in the right places but somehow miss the spark that expresses the individuality of the sitter. I doubt that anyone can tell you how to do it, but practice should help. If it doesn't, you can go back to landscapes.

There are two essentials for painting watercolor portraits: knowledge of how to draw the head and good control of watercolor technique. In painting a portrait, keep your eyes and mind open in studying the sitter's face. Look to see what's really there, not what you assume ought to be there. Watch for the relaxed expressive moment and try to get it down before you have forgotten it. Notice the gradations in skin tones and the way the shadows and highlights define the planes of the face. As a rule, you can leave the background till last, using it to heighten or tone down the colors in the face if necessary, as mentioned in the section on Keyed Color.

There is of course much more that could be said about watercolor portraiture, enough to fill a whole book in fact. These few suggestions are meant only to stimulate your interest in the subject and to encourage you to try it for yourself.

Portrait of Robert P. Tristram Coffin BY ELIOT O'HARA

COURTESY BOWDOIN COLLEGE MUSEUM OF ART, BRUNSWICK, MAINE

Composition, Design, and Related Matters

EVERY PICTURE you have painted has been a composition of some kind—good, bad, or indifferent. You have selected certain elements from those available and arranged them on the paper in some sort of relation to each other. If the design of the composition was satisfying, you may have turned out a pretty good picture, assuming that nothing went seriously wrong with the painting of it. If the design was unsatisfactory, you were probably strangely dissatisfied with the picture even if your technical handling of the brush and paints was never better.

Most artists have, or soon develop, an intuitive eye for design relationships, and most laymen react—without knowing why—to certain relationships of lines and areas. Whether a picture is a minutely detailed realistic representation of an actual scene or a nonobjective color pattern, the subject—or lack of it—is of less importance than the disposition on the paper or canvas of lines and spaces, colors and values.

Having said that much, you might expect a series of rules or formulas to follow. Well, if you go looking for rules, you can find them. In fact, some mathematically minded geniuses have devoted lifetimes to working out perfect proportions for all occasions. The only trouble is you can't paint good pictures by mathematical rules. If you are given to that sort of thing, you might go around analyzing successful paintings and then exclaiming, "See, it works out exactly to my formula!" But if you start with the formula and try to project it into a painting, the result is almost bound to be dull, sterile, and pointless.

The only way you can really discover the elements of good design for yourself is to study critically your own work and that of other artists. Pay attention to those paintings you think are awful as well as to those you like, and try to figure out why some things work and others don't.

Try not to jump to conclusions. If you make up your own little rules and formulas on the basis of too little knowledge and experience, you may brush yourself into a corner from which you will never get out. If you keep an open mind, you will learn a lot more and have a lot more fun.

Some of the many elements that are involved in composition and design are discussed more fully in the following pages. Analyze the paintings you see in terms of these elements, try the exercises suggested, and apply what you learn to your future work.

Dust and Limestone BY ELIOT O'HARA

Making Space Recede

Unless you restrict yourself to nonobjective painting or flat decorative design, you need to find ways to create distance or depth within your pictures. The use of light and shadow to define form is a beginning. The next step is to make objects appear to recede into space. There's more than one way to do it—as you've probably discovered—and in most pictures you use a combination of these techniques.

1. You can place distant objects above nearer ones—as primitives and children usually do—and the viewer will assume that the higher objects are farther away.

2. You can follow the rules of linear perspective, which you probably learned in simplified form in grade school. The basic rule is that distant objects appear smaller and nearer to the eye level or horizon than objects nearer the viewer. Some painters, from the Renaissance on, have been carried away with exercises in scientific perspective, but most artists use it more freely, obeying its exact rules only when they choose to. Few of the paintings in this book adhere strictly to scientific perspective. Even in very realistic scenes, certain perspective lines are likely to be distorted for the purpose of design or emphasis.

3. You can follow the rule for aerial or atmospheric perspective stated by Leonardo da Vinci that distant objects look paler, bluer,

The Adoration of the Magi BY SANDRO BOTTICELLI

COURTESY THE NATIONAL GALLERY OF ART, WASHINGTON, D. C. (MELLON COLLECTION)

Botticelli and other Renaissance painters could use the rules of linear and aerial perspective with scientific precision when they wished to, but often violated them to emphasize some other aspect of composition.

and less detailed. This rule works even in paintings that are quite abstract. Colors in themselves appear to recede or advance, and pale blues are inclined to recede no matter how they are used. In *The Red Fish House* on page 35, the distant mountains, which are painted pale blue, appear far more remote than the dark green foliage in the middle distance, although both areas are on about the same horizontal line. In the more abstract *Along the Seine*, on page 152, the vague blue towers are clearly distant from the deep blue, sharply drawn roofs of the central buildings.

4. You can make use of Paul Cézanne's observation that when one object overlaps another, one must be in front of the other. Cézanne didn't invent this one—it's been used since antiquity—but he did apply it in a new way, in combination with advancing and receding colors and a disregard for traditional perspective. You can apply it any way you want to.

Scale

One of the basic elements of any composition is scale, the relative proportion of objects within the picture frame. If you are painting a realistic scene, the basic rules of linear perspective will help to some extent to establish the scale of secondary objects in relation to the main feature of your subject. However, no rules will help as much as personal observation. If the main feature is a house, for instance, the size of the car in the driveway should appear in proper realistic scale to the house. If the car appears too large, the house may look like a child's playhouse or even a doll house. If the car appears too small, it may dwindle from Cadillac to Volkswagen to scale-model toy.

Besides establishing realistic-appearing relationships, scale can be very useful in making one area appear larger or smaller for emphasis. This gets into distortion, however, which we will take up later. Meantime, try this exercise. Paint two pictures of the same imaginary scene, perhaps a landscape with a house on a hill as the main element of the composition. Both pictures should be as identical in drawing, color, and proportion as you can make them. Now, in one picture add some object or element that will make the main feature seem very small. To the other, add something to make the principal feature appear very large.

Spotting

The disposition of areas, and their size, shape, and relation to each other is often more important to the success of a picture than the subject. If you could learn a list of rules and then apply them like a computer, everything might be easy. However, this is a realm rich in alternatives and your only dependable—and sometimes not too dependable—guide is your own taste and personal choice.

You can begin your study of spotting by looking over an ordinary deck of playing cards and considering which arrangements of spots are most pleasing and which least. Compare the ace of spades and the ace of clubs, for instance. Each is a simple black spot in the middle of a white vertical. My own preference would be for the ace of clubs because the size of the spot seems better related to the size of the card. Now look at the two of spades. Do you agree that the two spots should be closer together? How about the eight of diamonds? It reminds me of painters who fill their pictures with "things" rather than arranging individual elements to create a satisfying composition.

After you've analyzed the spotting faults in a deck of cards, try the following exercise to help develop your ability to spot areas of light and dark in interesting ways. Cut up pieces of white paper to about the size of playing cards and experiment with placing spots within a rectangle. The spots can be cut from black, gray, and colored papers in many different sizes and shapes. Or you can paint them on, or use crayons to color them.

Try placing a single black spot on a blank paper first. You will probably find that if it is not exactly in the middle, you will like it better. Now try several cards, each with one spot, but vary the sizes and shapes of the spots. You will always like one better than the others, and it is important to decide for yourself the reason for your choice.

Use a number of spots of various sizes and shapes cut from black paper and experiment with placing them in different quantities and different locations on one rectangle. Then add some gray spots and experiment with combinations of different value as well as different size.

This practice of cutting out shapes and trying them out on a background is good exercise in planning a painting. If you're not

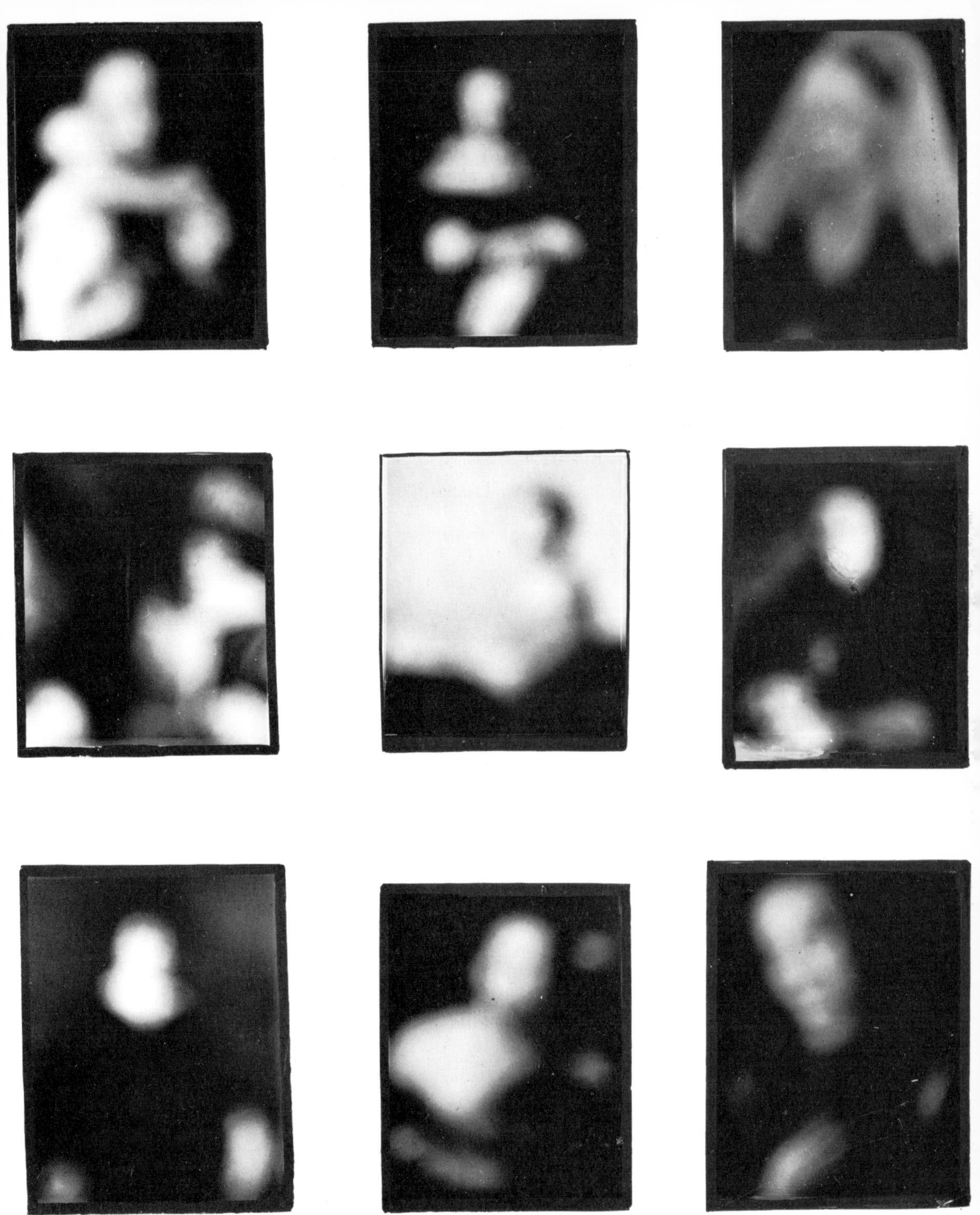

Interest in the subject itself sometimes makes it difficult to study the spotting of lights and darks in a realistic painting, but the out-of-focus reproductions above clearly reveal this design element in the group of old masters reproduced in the usual way on page 129.

sure just where to place a figure or a barn or any other element in a picture, cut out a paper shape and move it around on your sketch until you make up your mind where it should go. You might decide to leave it out altogether, or to make it larger or smaller.

After you have practiced with spots for a while, combine a line and two spots in various ways. Place them instinctively, by feeling rather than plan, and then try to figure out which ones you prefer and why.

Next try arrangements of horizontal stripes. Make them all run parallel straight across the rectangle, but vary their width and values. Then analyze them. Do you find the ones of equal width annoying? Why?

Think of these exercises in terms of designing the composition of a painting. The arrangements of spots and lines are pleasing and annoying for the same reasons that the arrangements of lines and spaces, values and colors are attractive or disturbing in a watercolor.

Now criticize some of your old pictures on a basis of spotting and arrangement. Re-do some of them changing the proportions and arrangement of elements in the picture to eliminate monotony and to achieve better balance.

The paintings opposite are all from the National Gallery of Art, Washington, D. C. From left to right: (top row) *Madonna and Child* by Correggio (?), from the Kress Collection; *Portrait of a Lady with an Ostrich Feather Fan* by Rembrandt van Rjn, from the Widener Collection; *Portrait of a Lady* by Rogier van der Weyden, from the Mellon Collection; (middle row) *A Young Girl with a Flute* by Jan Vermeer, from the Widener Collection; *The Lacemaker* by Jan Vermeer, from the Mellon Collection; *Sir Brian Tuke* by Hans Holbein the Younger, from the Mellon Collection; (bottom row) *Portrait of a Man* by Frans Hals, from the Widener Collection; *A Young Woman with a Parrot* by Giovanni Battista Tiepolo, from the Kress Collection; *Portrait of a Youth* by Sandro Botticelli, the Mellon Collection.

DROIT ET
AVANT

The Path of Vision

When you first view a picture, your mind does not necessarily grasp at once all that is to be seen there. The eye cannot see or report to the brain all things at once. It can look directly at only one thing at a time. So the eye moves over the scene, traveling from one spot to another. Attention lingers here or there as it finds something to note until it covers the whole area—or loses interest completely.

There has to be a starting point for this path of the eye. The attention will first be attracted to any bright-colored area or to some spot that presents a strong contrast of dark or light. If there is a choice between several of these entrances into the picture, the eye will choose the lower. If the painting is an all-over pattern of equally attracting elements, the eye will enter at the middle of the bottom edge. This is because we have trained our eyes to sweep from our toes upward toward the horizon. Whether a child crawling or an adult walking or driving, our eyes automatically search for and register any obstruction.

Habit also makes us look toward the right more easily than toward the left, probably because we read print from left to right.

The eye takes these directions, however, only when other conditions are equal. Most of the time it moves from one element or area to the nearest one that attracts it. The eye will seek out any figure, or even a church or house, as pertaining to people, or it will jump across the paper in the direction in which a figure is looking or pointing. It follows lines or rows of spots. It moves along furrows of a field or any other kind of stripes rather than across them. It roves quickly over smooth textures and more slowly over rough ones, and it pauses to reconnoiter anything unusual. It passes more easily from one object to another which is similar in color or shape. It travels not only up and down and crossways, but into the picture along planes, or flat surfaces, and out again. It will bank a corner on a plane and bounce back from a diagonal barrier.

This explains why many artists paint skies that have clouds in the form of an arch, and why others like to cut off all four corners of a picture. These banked corners are the easiest way to keep the observer's eye within the picture and thus hold his interest.

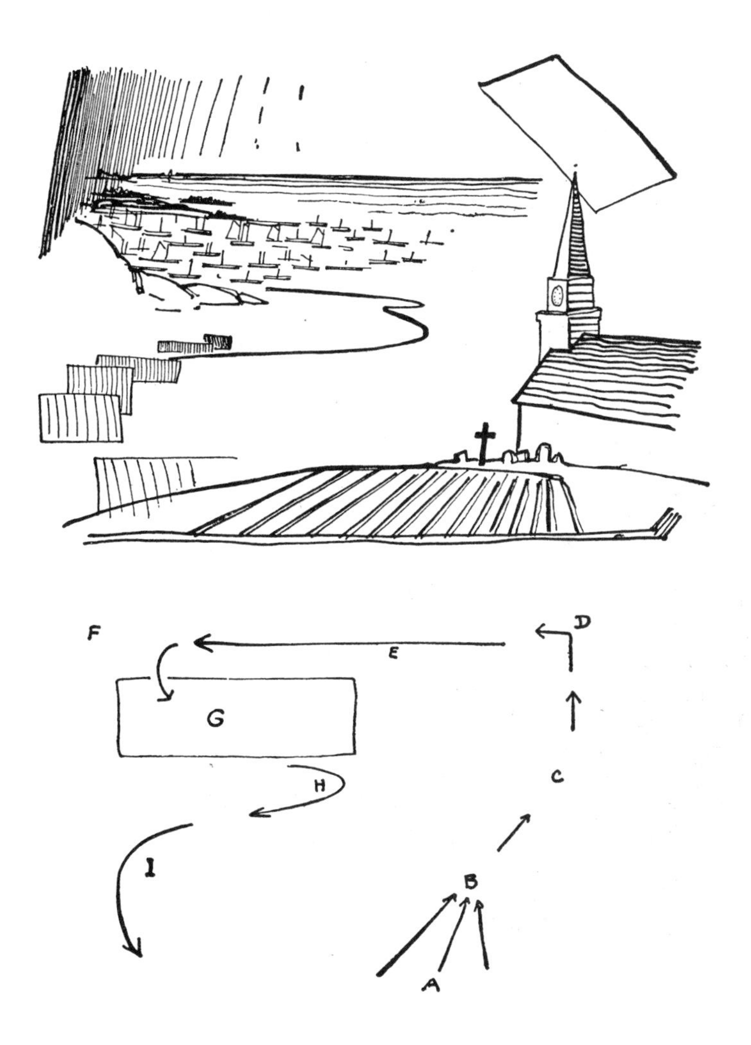

The diagram traces the path of vision in the sketch above it. The plowed field, A, first catches the eye and carries it to the cross, B, whereupon it moves up the church, C, and off the end of the steeple. It is prevented from going out of the top of the picture by a banked corner, D, which might be a cloud or a tree. The line of least resistance then makes it follow the horizon, E. It is prevented from going out of the left-hand side of the frame by the darkening and thickening of the sky. After being thus slowed down, it catches on the dark islands below. The rough hatching of the surface, G, is intended to hold the eye for some time before it follows along the edge of the beach, H, and is picked up by a succession of similar areas, I, which might be billboards, houses, or other elements in the landscape. Then it returns to the starting point. This is a rather obvious plan such as any beginner might attempt. With practice you will find more subtle ways of leading the eye where you want it to go.

Pelion upon Ossa
BY ELIOT O'HARA

Try to analyze the path your own eye follows in looking at *Pelion upon Ossa* before studying the path traced in the diagram at right.

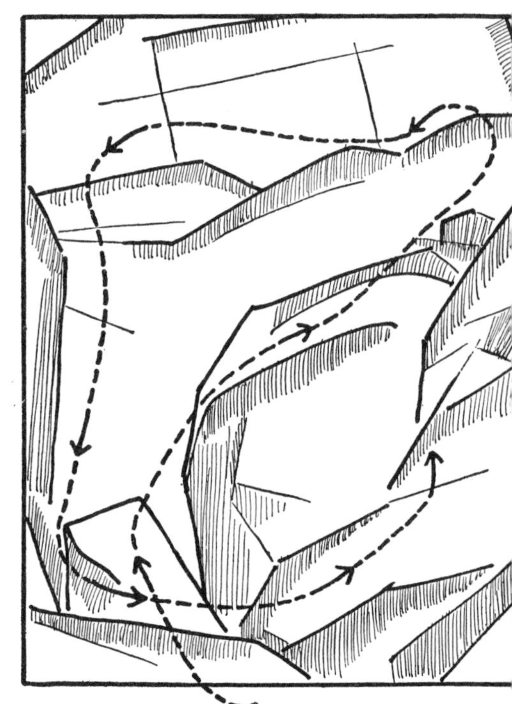

Frequently, an unconscious obstruction is placed in the path of vision by fencing the observer out of the picture with a horizontal band straight across the foreground. Such a line should always have a break in it somewhere or a cross line to bridge it.

As an experiment, take a new magazine containing many unfamiliar pictures—photographs will do as well for this as paintings. Open the magazine at random and for a minute let your attention go where it will. Now remember just what your takeoff point was. Why did you start there? Remember just what route you took and analyze this route, explaining why your eye followed it. There is always a reason for each move, and you should be able to figure it out.

After your analysis, you can decide whether the artist dictated your route, or whether your eye simply strayed on impulse.

Since every picture is bound to have a "path of the eye," whether the artist intends it or not, you should plan it before you start to paint. It isn't necessary, or perhaps possible, to think out the entire path of vision at once. It will grow as you plan your composition, a bit at a time. The middle or end may be set down before the starting point.

When you first attempt to work with a definite path of the eye in mind, you will probably tend to be self-conscious about it and choose the most obvious kind. The path should not be a summons to follow and look, but the most subtle kind of suggestion that there is more to see in that direction. The observer likes to feel that he is choosing his path rather than being driven down it.

Directional Signals

In planning a path of vision you found that the eye will follow certain lines and shapes. Wedge shapes, for instance, are as strongly directional as arrows; so are curves, straight lines, or any series of identical, or even similar, elements. Watch for these directional signals. They can be very useful in focusing attention where you want it, but they can also lead the eye right out of the picture, never to return, if you don't provide stop signals or detours. What form these traffic signals take will depend on the nature of your picture.

Look over the paintings you have done and identify some of the more obvious directional signals—wedge-shaped clouds, the bend of a river, a tree-lined road, a row of houses. The list could be endless. Now try to judge for yourself whether the directional pull is too strong for the balance of the composition. If you find your eye riveted on one spot for too long, you may have aimed too many arrows toward your center of attention. A less obvious approach would probably make the whole picture more interesting. If your eye keeps wandering off to one side and out of the picture completely, you may have two or more strong directional signals pointing that way with nothing to stop or counteract them. Try to figure out some way to hold the eye within the picture area. A wedge of cloud or a strong shadow form pointing inward might be enough to lead the eye back in toward the center. The strong vertical of a telephone pole might stop the eye from wandering out of another picture. The trunk and curving branches of a tree could provide a frame for a third. These are very obvious examples. Study the paintings reproduced in this book—and any other paintings you have a chance to see—for more subtle directional signals.

North Michigan Avenue, Chicago BY ELIOT O'HARA

The main boulevard would lead the eye right out of the picture at the top left were it not for the heavy weight of the dark building and the counterpull of the light area to the right.

Balance

Any element in a composition that attracts the viewer's attention will disturb rather than interest him unless it is balanced by some counter element or elements. The attention-getting device may be a small spot of brilliant color, an area of unexpectedly light or dark value, a massive or unusual shape, a line or plane that pulls the eye in a definite direction, or a variation in texture. If this is satisfactorily balanced by some other element or combination of elements, the viewer enjoys—without necessarily thinking of it in such terms—the play of tensions within the picture. If it is not balanced, the viewer gets to keep the tension for himself. He may not know why he didn't like the picture, but suddenly he's bored, or restless, or is beginning to get a slight headache.

No one can tell you how to keep the tensions working within your picture. You have to figure it out for yourself each time you create a new composition. A small brilliant red spot—representing a figure, perhaps—might be balanced in one picture by an arbitrary thin red line and in another by a grayed rosy brick wall. Whether or not either of these arrangements would prove satisfactory would depend of course on their size and placement in relation to each other and to all the other elements of the composition.

It might be helpful to think of the composition as representing a seesaw with the fulcrum, or point of support, in dead center. Then visualize what would happen with objects of different weights in varying positions. For instance, one man might be balanced by two youngsters, or four small children, or a mother and child. The position of the weights in relation to the fulcrum would also affect the balance. This is an oversimplification, but it may help if you can think of such elements as color, value, line, and mass as having weights or strengths to be combined in a variety of interesting but balanced relationships.

Interacting Planes

When you look at a sheet of clean white watercolor paper, you see a flat surface, or two-dimensional plane, bounded by four sides. You can bend the paper to form concave and convex curves, or even a cylinder, but the surface remains one plane. However, if you draw a line across the flat surface of the paper from one side to another, something happens. As you stare at the paper, you find it increasingly difficult to see it as a flat piece of paper with a line drawn across it. The line creates two planes; it is the place where two surfaces meet. Both planes may appear flat at first, but as you look at them, their joining place will appear to recede or advance and the two places will form an angle which appears either to lie within the paper's boundaries or to extrude out toward you.

Old Gables II BY LYONEL FEININGER

COURTESY CURRIER GALLERY OF ART, MANCHESTER, N. H.

Architectural elements are transformed into shifting planes of transparent color in many of Feininger's distinctive paintings.

If you paint the two areas with graded washes, you can increase the illusion of dimension and can even control the apparent movement. If the washes are graded from a light or cool color at the edges to a dark or warm color at the center, the corner will come toward you. If the dark or warm tones are on the outer edges and the light or cool tones toward the center of the paper, the corner will recede. However, if flat washes are used, particularly if strongly contrasting colors are painted in the adjoining areas, the corner will continue to move in and out, probably with annoying frequency. This very jumpy effect might be just right for a picture of a teen-age dance party. For more restful subjects you will probably want to avoid it.

Planes not only advance and recede, creating movement in depth, back into the painting and out toward the viewer, they also attract and repel each other, creating surface movement from top to bottom and side to side. If you want to demonstrate this, take two squares of cardboard or two sheets of paper. Hold them flat, one in each hand, face up. In that position they seem mutually agreeable, or at least neutral. Now tip them slowly toward each other, their bottom edges about a foot apart. They seem conscious of each other and you can sense a tension developing between them. In certain positions, tipped slightly toward each other, for example, they seem to offer mutual support or balance. Tipped away from each other, there is something like the tension of a tug of war. If both cards are tipped in the same direction, you have the uneasy feeling they will both collapse. With both cards upright, their flat sides facing, they seem in balance, but move one toward the other and you can almost feel the resistance as they seem to repel each other. Now turn both flat sides toward you and move the cards toward each other edgewise. There is no problem at all. They approach, and move in front or in back or away from each other without hindrance.

The interaction of planes can be an important element in any composition. It can create tensions that keep the eye constantly interested as it moves from one plane to another, from side to side, and back and forth within the picture.

In straightforward representational pictures this interplay is usually disguised by realistic details. Therefore, to get the feel of these relationships, try painting a series of pictures in which the

Shipyard, Fort Lauderdale BY ELIOT O'HARA

realistic elements are flattened, distorted, or thrown away completely in the interest of a design based entirely on planes and the relationships between them.

It might be easier for a start to base your first attempts on paintings you have already done. Choose those that seem to offer a good starting point for experiments with surfaces and work out your new versions in pencil sketches before starting to paint. Think of the picture area as a cube, limited in depth as well as width, and keep all of your planes within that cube.

As a general rule, use dark tones for planes that are near you and keep those that are farther away light. However, as you experiment, you will discover that by overlapping surfaces it is sometimes possible to make a light plane edge appear to be this side of a dark one. If you make some of your planes transparent, you

The Joe Doaks House—PLANES

Analysis of the balance of tensions and planes in the picture above.

can show one plane behind another, each surface suggesting movement in a different direction.

In working this way, you don't have to feel restricted by what you see or what you know to be true. You can show the far side of a solid or the back of a hill if you decide you want to, or you can continue a roof plane right on into the sky. You can disclose truth the eye cannot see—or, if you're in that kind of mood, you can impose untruths on the unsuspecting viewer. One picture may be composed of recognizable surfaces only slightly distorted and rearranged, another may be quite abstract, a picture in which interweaving surfaces lose their identity as they become elements of design.

AN EXERCISE IN PAINTING PLANES

In painting *The Joe Doaks House* on the opposite page, the realistic use of shadows, colors, and textures was ignored. Colors and values were chosen not because they suggested the local color of the area being painted, but because they created an effect that was warm or cool, light or dark, advancing or receding.

The lawn, for instance, is warmer and darker nearby, paler and cooler farther away. The rounded forms of tree trunks, foliage, figures, or other objects are expressed in straight edges and planes. The finished picture is not a reproduction of the scene, but an invitation to the viewer to participate in the play of tensions created by interacting planes. The front corner of the roof and porch, for example, establishes the edge of a plane extending to the right and the viewer must decide where the plane ends. To compensate this tension, there is an arbitrary left-facing plane at the far right, which could be interpreted as a telephone pole or part of a tree.

A balance of tensions was worked out between the flattened planes of the roof, the sky, and the lawn, as the arrows in the analysis of the painting indicate. The planes of the figure and the porch steps have been balanced by the foreground planes.

The Distorted View

Distortion isn't a bad word unless the distortion is meaningless or an indication of the artist's lack of control. In painting any picture from nature you have to select and rearrange the forms and colors you actually see to produce a composition that satisfies you. Even the most faithful reproduction of the scene will be one artist's view of it and to some extent distorted.

Distortion is one of your chief means of expressing your viewpoint about the subject. By changing colors, values, lines, shapes, sizes, and relationships you can express a mood, comment on an attitude, put forth an idea, or reveal what you hope is a new truth about an old-hat subject.

The Feast of Pure Reason BY JACK LEVINE

COURTESY MUSEUM OF MODERN ART, NEW YORK

By exaggerating the size and shape of the hands and faces of the three figures, Levine has emphasized their grossness and made a personal comment on politicians.

Cerro de la Silla, Monterrey BY ELIOT O'HARA

Coastal Cypress BY ELIOT O'HARA

The Joe Doaks House—STATIC

To create a feeling of peaceful calm, muted tones of green, gray, and brown were substituted for the clear bright colors of the original realistic painting. Wherever possible, diagonal lines were changed to sleepy horizontals and staid verticals. A soft mistiness was suggested with wet blending.

The Joe Doaks House—DYNAMIC

To establish a dynamic mood, colors and values were made dissonant and contrasty. The house was painted bright orange to fight the brilliant blue of the sky. Horizontals and verticals were tilted, angles and edges sharpened, and lazy curves became violent swoops. The forward lean of the figures implies energetic movement.

How you do it is up to you. Children, for instance, usually enlarge whatever it is that interests them most in a picture. Many artists do the same—though hopefully with more control. Gaston Lachaise, the sculptor noted for his bronzes of buxom, hippy women, enlarged the specifically feminine aspects of the female figure to express his view of the personification of woman. Figures are often made taller and slimmer, with small heads and frail hands, to express graceful, ethereal, or spiritual qualities. In Jack Levine's *The Feast of Pure Reason,* the figures are caricatured as extremely short, squat, heavy-jowled and heavy-handed to suggest grossness. In painting landscapes, it is common to exaggerate the height of a mountain, as I did in *Cerro de la Silla, Monterrey.*

Another form of distortion is the use of lines, planes, and directions to express a feeling about the subject. Diagonal lines, angular planes, sweeping curves, and other strong directional signals produce tensions and movement that create a dynamic composition suggesting action. Even if the subject is just the old Joe Doaks house sitting quietly in its little green yard, you can tell from the sharp angle of the roof and the menacing planes of the trees in front that "something" is about to happen. On the other hand, if the composition is dominated by sleepy horizontals, lazy curves, staid and upright verticals, the scene is bound to be restful and quiet, a nice place to come home to after a hard day's work. Be careful though that you don't put the viewer to sleep.

You have already played with the use of selective color—another aspect of distortion—so you know that color can be used to create whatever feeling the painter wants to suggest.

As an experiment, do several new versions of your old paintings, making each one say something different about the subject. If you use the Joe Doaks house, for example, you might emphasize its commonplaceness in one painting, make it a deserted house in another, find a spiritual quality in it in a third. One note of caution: Don't try to make any one painting say too many things.

Rhythm

Although most of us think first of music when we think of rhythm, we frequently use the word in a much broader sense, applying it to all the arts, to speech, to patterns of living, to the beat of our own heart. The dictionary also takes the broad view, defining rhythm as a flow or movement characterized by the basically regular recurrence of similar or identical elements alternating with opposite or different elements.

In painting, the flow is the movement of the eye as it follows the path of vision. If the colors, values, lines, planes, volumes, and spaces are well composed, the eye will move easily and rhythmically from one area to another, but if there are unresolved tensions, barriers that can't be hurdled, colors out of key, or other distracting elements, the rhythm will be broken and the composition will seem to fall apart.

Brunete, Spanish War, 1938

BY LUIS QUINTANILLA

COURTESY CROSBY GALLERY OF ART

Motif #1 in this rhythmic composition is the angle of the roof. A small curve of arch (#2) and a crisscross line (#3) are minor accompanying motifs. None of the three is ever repeated exactly, but as the eye moves in and about the picture, it is pleased to discover unexpected similarities.

White Gazelles

BY OLIVE RUSH

The graceful curves and delicate coloring of the white gazelles are echoed with many rhythmic variations in the background forms of rocks, hills, and foliage.

Every picture has a rhythm of its own which is related to the mood or viewpoint that is being expressed. It is established by the dominant elements of the composition—characteristic colors, curves, planes, or whatever—which are repeated or echoed at certain intervals throughout the composition. In some pictures the repetition may be quite obvious and the rhythm may itself be an important factor in the composition. The painter might even consciously try to evoke a particular kind of music or dance rhythm. In most paintings, however, the rhythm will be much less obvious. If it's there, you won't think about it—any more than you think about breathing until you find you're gasping for air.

To become more conscious of the subtle play of rhythm in the organization of a painting, spend some time analyzing every picture you see, much as I've analyzed *White Gazelles* by Olive Rush and *Brunete, Spanish War, 1938* by Luis Quintanilla, then plan a picture in which rhythm is your main interest. Look for some motif or theme that lends itself to repetition with variations—the curve of an automobile fender, the color of a flower, or whatever interests you. Search for unexpected ways to repeat the theme, to vary it, to barely suggest it, then to repeat it again. Don't make the repetitions too obvious or the viewer may be bored. Let him enjoy his own cleverness when he discovers that this spot of red is repeated over here as a thin line and there as a series of dots, and is echoed softly as a darker value in that shadow area.

Restraint

It's rarely possible in one picture to say all there is to say about the subject. The best we can hope to do is to make one clear statement that represents our view at the time of painting. Tomorrow or next week we may see the same subject in a different light, may come to it in a different mood, but today we see it "this way"—so that's the way to paint it. Sometimes, though, we find the subject so fascinating or so complicated that we don't have a clear idea of just what we do want to say about it. We know—or think we know—too much about it and we can't bear to leave anything out. The picture that results from that kind of mood is likely to say everything so badly that it says nothing at all. No one paints masterpieces every time out, and while we're experimenting and searching there

Light Keeper's House BY HOWARD GILES

COLLECTION OF EDWARD POWERS

The Amishman's Wagon BY ELIOT O'HARA

are bound to be noble experiments gone wrong. Too often, though, our failures are not so noble; we're just guilty of "gossiping with paint"—of talking aimlessly when we have nothing to say, of rambling on, repeating ourselves, and boring everyone else to death. Even very good painters are guilty of such lapses from time to time, so it's a good idea to keep in mind the virtue of restraint.

Restraint is one of the essential qualities of a good performance in almost any field—whether it be painting, writing, acting, singing, preaching, selling, or whatever. It is not inhibition or lack of vitality, but the exercise of intelligent control over all the factors involved so that nothing important is missing and nothing unnecessary is added.

In a work of art, whether the subject is exuberant, colorful, earthy, simple, spiritual, elegant, quiet, or loud, the viewer should feel that there is a reserve of power barely touched, that there is more to the subject and to the painter's knowledge of it than is at first apparent.

Of course there has to be enough in the picture to stimulate the viewer's awareness of those hidden reserves. If the picture is too restrained, the result may be sterile and dull. It's a toss-up which is worse—the run-on talker or the uncommunicative bore.

As an experiment in restraint, try painting some rather complicated subject—a town seen from a hill, a distant group of buildings, a forest, or a building with much architectural detail, such as one of the overdecorated gingerbread houses of the turn of the century. In painting the picture, try to imply the wealth of detail without actually putting it in. If you paint a town, try to get the feeling of its being a town rather than an accumulation of houses. The picture of the ornate building might create a mood of nostalgia or make a biting comment on changing tastes, but it need not serve as a carpenter's guide for the fretwork.

The Devil's Thumb, Alaska BY ELIOT O'HARA

Stony Squaw Mountain BY ELIOT O'HARA

Along the Seine BY ELIOT O'HARA

Abstract and Nonobjective Painting

THEY HAVE both been around for quite a while now, but there is still a great deal of confusion about abstract and nonobjective painting. Although the words are often used interchangeably, particularly in reference to nonobjective work, the words are not synonymous. Both types of painting are more concerned with design than with pictorial elements, but the abstraction often has at least its roots in reality while the nonobjective bears no intentional relation to any recognizable object.

Some abstractions get so far from their source that you would never know they had one if it weren't for the title. In others the subject remains readily recognizable even though it is simplified or distorted for the sake of the design. In *Glacier,* on page 154, I created an abstract pattern based on a subject I had previously observed and painted in a more realistic manner. Without the title you might not recognize the subject and that might or might not

Abstraction BY JOHN D. MCLAUGHLIN

COURTESY BOWDOIN COLLEGE MUSEUM OF ART, BRUNSWICK, MAINE

McLaughlin eliminates every vestige of imagery and symbolism in his painting in order to achieve a totally abstract approach which he believes frees the viewer from distracting sensations and forces him to look within himself for understanding.

Glacier BY ELIOT O'HARA

WATERCOLOR
BY XAVIER GONZALEZ

affect your enjoyment of it. With the title, you at least know what I had in mind when I painted it. It seems possible that the original inspiration for the Xavier Gonzalez watercolor on page 154 was a ship, but since the artist hasn't given it a title, you can interpret it as you will. In *Old Gables II,* on page 137, Lyonel Feininger created an abstract arrangement of interweaving planes, but the row of medieval houses with which he started is still clearly visible. I reduced the details of *Fisherman's Wharf,* page 78, to the barest essentials, but you can recognize San Francisco landmarks in the scene if you look for them.

You may enjoy solving abstract picture puzzles, but if you try to find hidden objects in nonobjective paintings, you're on the wrong track. You may see them, just as you see the man in the moon, or lobster claws in the sky, or butterflies in an ink blot, but your discoveries will be of more interest to your psychoanalyst than to the painter. Nonobjective painting is like pure music that has no literary associations but exists only as an arrangement of sounds. Like such musical compositions, nonobjectives often are numbered rather than named. The artist is not trying to reproduce an image or to interpret a visual experience; he is putting together colors, values, textures, lines, planes, volumes, thrusts, tensions, movements, or whatever painting or design elements he chooses, in a way that gives him a thrill and—if he's lucky—excites his audience. There are no rules except those he makes himself. His painting technique may be as precise as that of the most conservative academician or he may experiment with whatever new and unorthodox materials and techniques occur to him. The results may be coolly geometric, intricate and detailed, or wild, colorful, and explosive. They can also be deadly dull. It depends on the painter.

If you have experimented with planes, distortion, selective color, and other approaches to creative painting discussed in previous sections, you have already begun to work toward abstraction. Now is the time to go further and try nonobjective painting. As a starting point, place any line or brushmark of color on the paper, then expand it into an organized composition. Once you have made a stroke on the paper, you are committed to relate succeeding strokes and lines to it. You can allow your imagination free rein, uninhibited by reality, but you still have to maintain control of the design.

If you find it difficult to free yourself from a factual subject in painting, either because you are not familiar with nonobjective paintings or because you are antagonistic to them, make a point of searching them out. Don't depend on magazine and book illustrations, which can only give you a vague idea of what a painting is really like, but look for them in galleries and museums and really study them. Don't reject them until you've had a chance to get used to them. Then try to decide which ones you like best and which least. As with landscapes, or seascapes, or portraits, you're bound to like some better than others, but in this case your preference will have nothing to do with the subject. Pay attention to your reactions and try to analyze them. You may learn more than you would expect about the emotional effect of pure design. You can apply what you learn to the painting of your own nonobjectives if you like, or you can transfer that knowledge to the interpretation of any kind of subject you choose.

A Variety of Approaches

IF YOU have been following the suggestions throughout this book, you should by now have tried all sorts of manners of expression. Perhaps one or two of them have proved a starting point for more personal experiments of your own. That's exactly what they were meant to do. But perhaps you have latched onto some gimmick like rough brushing or calligraphy or wet blending, and you're very busy making it your own. That may not be such a good idea. Limiting yourself to a few technical tricks can easily lead you up a blind alley. You may think you're developing a personal style when you're just settling for a formula that takes all the creativity out of creation. This can be especially dangerous to your artistic development if your formula pictures become popular and sell. More than one potentially brilliant painter has ended up in a well-established rut.

As to how to avoid such a fate—settling in a rut, that is; hardly anyone wants to avoid selling pictures—one of the best ways is to experiment with many different approaches to seeing and painting the same subject. You can take any subject that interests you—a commonplace still life or landscape will do—and interpret it in dozens of styles, techniques, and moods. In the pictures reproduced opposite and on pages 158-159, for instance, I have taken a house that could be down the street from the Joe Doaks place and painted it in twelve different ways, ranging from a straightforward, but somewhat simplified, realistic manner to several fairly abstract approaches. It could have been done in many other ways as well. The point is to remind you that there is no necessary relationship between the subject you paint and the way you paint it.

12 Ways of Looking at One Subject

The watercolor above shows a house just down the street from the Joe Doaks place. It's a fairly accurate picture of the house although I've left out a lot of nonessential detail —the first step toward abstraction.

The house looks different as the light changes from morning to night and from sunny to overcast. The paintings on the right show three of many possible ways of representing the house with different arrangements of areas of light and dark value.

Surface textures were emphasized in this version. After experimenting on a separate sheet, I decided to use rough brushing for the lawn, whisk strokes for the pine tree, small brushstrokes for the tree trunk, and white lines made through waxed paper for the louvered windows and the aluminum roof.

Wet-blended edges give this version a soft-focus quality.

Vague areas of selective color are identified and tied together with calligraphy.

Lost-and-found edges force the viewer to help create this picture.

Tensions are established between planes within the picture cube.

Unpainted intervals of white paper dominate this composition.

Distortion creates a dynamic mood with forceful diagonals.

Distortion creates a feeling of tranquillity with quiet horizontals and verticals.

A Final Word

WATERCOLOR and the related water-soluble mediums have become more and more popular in recent years. They lend themselves easily to experimental work in a variety of techniques, and for the most part they are as permanent as oils. In earlier times painters had to devise and mix their own paints, but we have chemists who have produced new pigments and vehicles far superior to those of the Renaissance.

In the world of painting, however, the problems of techniques and materials are of relatively minor importance. It isn't the chemistry of the paint—or even its permanence—that matters. The physical durability of a work of art is of far less interest than its artistic merit.

Let us forget about astonishing the world with tricks of craftsmanship and concentrate on developing our talents as disciplined but creative artists. Almost anyone can learn technique. The problem is to use that technique to place colors, areas, and lines on the paper or canvas in a way that will give the viewer—and particularly the artist himself—the greatest possible emotional thrust.

While you are still experimenting with techniques and ways of expressing yourself, you should begin to send entries to the juried art shows nearest you. It will help you to find your place in the world of painting. You should realize, however, that a rejection is nothing to be dejected about, nor an acceptance anything to warrant more than a momentary glow of satisfaction. Plenty of good pictures have been thrown out of the best exhibitions, and plenty of very bad ones hung. Juries do queer things when they have looked at pictures all day. There are always differences of opinion, disagreements, and compromises. Each juror, had he been the sole judge, would probably have picked an entirely different set of pictures. So if your first few entries come back rejected, don't give up. The next jury may be more agreeable.

Remember, though, that it really doesn't matter whether any jury or critic likes your work. There is no constituted authority—although there are many self-appointed ones. In the end, you are the creator, the appreciator, and the final judge and jury of your own pictures. You should have more fun painting them than anyone can ever hope to have just looking at them.

Supplementary Films Available

Many of the points covered in this book are demonstrated in a series of 16mm films, all in color and with sound tracks. The following films are available for purchase or rental from Encyclopaedia Britannica Films, Wilmette, Ill.:

"Brush Techniques," 400 ft.
"Painting Reflections in Water," 400 ft.
"Painting an Abstraction," 400 ft.
"Color Keying in Art and Living," 400 ft.
"Painting Trees with Eliot O'Hara," 600 ft.
(Best Art Film award, Cleveland, 1954).
"Painting with Calligraphy," 400 ft.
(Certificate of Merit, Cleveland, 1956).
"Oriental Brushwork," 600 ft.
"Painting Clouds," 500 ft.
"Painting Crowds of People," 400 ft.
"Rhythm in Paint," 400 ft.
"Painting Shadows," 400 ft.
"Drawing a Portrait," 400 ft.
"Painting a Portrait," 400 ft.